the
daily dose
by Mitch Anthony

240 STORIES
AND IDEAS THAT
MOTIVATE AND INSPIRE

Mitch Anthony's books are available at special quantity discounts to use as premiums and sales promotions, or for use in corporate training programs.

For more information, please call:
(507) 282-2723, or write to
Advisor Insights Inc. at
P.O. Box 34, Rochester, MN 55903

www.mitchanthony.com

Managing Editor: Debbie Anthony
Interior Design: Greg Wimmer
Cover Design: Greg Wimmer

ISBN: 0-9727523-0-7

Dedication

This book is dedicated to all the wonderful people I have met in my life and career – those who are determined to live positive lives and do so by speaking positive words to everyone they meet. A quality life is a matter of direction, not feeling, and I am indebted to so many who have taught me by example how to move in the right direction. You know who you are – and how rare you are.

Contents

Acknowledgments . . . . . **viii**

Preface . . . . **ix**

PART ONE
Attitude Adjustment

The Attitude Instrument. 2
The Greatest Pitcher of All Time . 3
Happiness Is Being Happy 4
The Ladder of Achievement 5
Getting Started 6
Ketchup 7
I Could've Given More 8
Tragically Comic 9
The Present 10
Time for a Time Out! 11
Accidental Tourists 12
Weigh-In 13
The "Kee-Ya" 14
Private Courage 15
Asking, "Why?" 16
An "I Can't" Attitude 17
Smile, If You Can 18
The Town that Wasn't 19
Blind Optimism 20
Hidden Opportunities 21
That Winning Ingredient 22
The Moody Blues 23
The "H-A-L-T Rule" 24
Dog Eat Dog 25
When is Enough, Enough? 26
What You Say to Yourself 27
Comfort Zones 28
Wisest of the Athenians 29
Constant Cultivation 30
The Greatest Power 31
Continuous Improvement 32
Words – The Attitude Food 33
Childlike Wonder 34
"Good Shot, Daddy!" 35
The CLOs 36
Three-Part Cure 37
Work for Play 38
For, Not Against 39
Rich with Happiness 40
Fired Up or Burned Out 41

Mind Your Body 42
Know What You Are Good At . . 43
More Than Two Sides 44
What Money Cannot Buy 45
At Your Own Expense 46
Ending the Guilt Trip 47
The Happiness Paradox 48
Working At Humor 49
Stay Until You Like It 50
"Can-Do" Attitudes 51
Happy at Work 52
No Whiners Allowed 53
New Tricks for Old Dogs 54
Resilience 55
The Human Frog 56
Power of Passion 57
Rolling the Dice 58
Heading North 59
Soul of the Job 60
Sure Beats Walking 61

PART TWO
Building Relationships

Things Aren't So Bad 64
First Things First 65
Four Words of Praise 66
How Do You Spell Love? 67
Let's Hope We're Man Enough 68
Soft Answer 69
Promise Keepers 70
The Time to Laugh 71
It's Great to be Great 72
Doing a Little More 73
Father's Day Cards 74
Maintenance Programs 75
Random Acts of Kindness 76
Timmy, You're a Man Now . . 77
Spilled Milk 78
What's in a Name? 79
Leaders Follow 80
Radiate Friendship 81
Keep It Simple 82
Pleasing Nobody 83
How You Treat Yourself 84

Rowing Together 85
Strength in Weakness 86
Simple Expectations 87
Mutual Respect 88
Test of Love 89
Emphatically Yours 90
Communicate 91
Lead, Don't Drive 92
The Debate Rule 93
Significant Others 94
Focus on Strengths 95
My Brother's Brother 96
The More, the Merrier 97
Careful About Assumptions . . 98
Sincerely 99
"I was Wrong" 100
Rattlesnakes and Earthquakes 101
Playful Spirits 102
No Ordinary People 103
Listen with Your Face 104
Just Think 105
Fishing and Hunting 106
The Empty Box 107
"How Are You?" 108
Sosa's Sign 109
Fighting Out 110
Give the Chickens
Their Space 111
Perfect Strangers 112
False Humility 113
Don't Argue with a Fool 114
Why Whales Jump 115
You See What You Look For . 116
Make the Most of the Moment 117
Leave It to the Birds 118
Remember Your "A-B-Cs" . . 119
Joy in Annoyances 120
Know What Matters 121
Time and Money 122
Showing Up 123

PART THREE
Fulfilling Your Potential
Practice, Practice, Practice . . 126

Expressing Who You Are . . . 127
Dream Days 128
The Real Contest 129
High Dives 130
Plateaus 131
Wish Upon a Star 132
Dragons 133
"Baby Steps" 134
Goals Are Easier Than
They First Appear 135
What Do You Know? 136
Falling Off Your Horse 137
Win Without Bragging;
Lose Without Excuse 138
The Harder You Work,
The More It Means 139
Rejection in the Garbage 140
The Mind Once Stretched . . . 141
Change Comes with
Dissatisfaction 142
You Know You Are Right . . . 143
Great Spirits 144
The Knuckle-Ballers 145
Where is the Ladder Leaning? 146
Be Yourself 147
"I Don't Do Windows" 148
Learning to Lose 149
Nice Try 150
Take Fun Seriously 151
You've Got a Dream 152
The Width and Depth 153
"Tryumph!" 154
The Good Old Days 155
Make Your Breaks 156
Ask the Right Person 157
Afraid to Ask 158
You Deserve Better 159
Programmed to Succeed 160
Delayed Gratification 161
Recognizing Ability 162
Those that Care the Least . . . 163
Write It Down 164
Your Reference Group 165
Easy to Fail 166

Declare Your Intentions 167
The Need to Think 168
Correct and Adjust 169
Big Dogs 170
Brilliant Mind – Broken Body 171
Define Your Destiny 172
Where Creativity Lies 173
A View From the Ridge 174
See the Big Picture 175
Astound Yourself 176
Energy vs. Talent 177
Reward Improvement 178
"What Do You Do?" 179
Malek's Law 180
Walk Like a Baby 181
Sweet Smell of Success 182
Adventures 183
You Have to Know
Who Knows 184

PART FOUR
Time-Tested Values

True North 186
Good Leaders 187
Glasses and Water 188
Anticipation / Realization . . . 189
You Cannot Fake Sincerity . . 190
Taking Time 191
Ben Franklin's
Simple Formula 192
Overnight Success 193
Live and Help Live 194
Self-Government 195
Light From Darkness 196
A Life of Risk 197
The Mighty Seed 198
Just Lucky 199
Small Beginnings 200
Real Character 201
Don't Get Even – Get Mad! . 202
The Extra Mile at
the Last Minute 203
Own Up 204
Wanted: Kindness 205

Churchill's Battle Plans 206
Remove the Welcome Mat . . 207
The Worst Can Bring
Out the Best 208
Old Dogs 209
Watching the Polls 210
Good Reminders 211
"Sweet 16" 212
100 and Counting 213
Door Openers 214
Fix It As Soon As You See It 215
What Lies Within You 216
Win by Losing 217
Get Your Hands Dirty 218
Passing the Test 219
Good Values Linger 220
Hang Onto Seeds 221
The Power of Humility 222
The Greatest Generation 223
From the Heart 224
New Priorities 225
"Awesome, Baby!" 226
Pictures for Daddy 227
Exercise of Prayer 228
Einsteinium Success 229
Your Second Job 230
That's the Truth, Teacher! . . . 231
Money Talks 232
Detecting Counterfeits 233
In Stitches 234
The Richest Legacy 235
Speed: The Enemy
of Progress? 236
EQ 237
Anonymous Angel 238
Heroes 239
Work Worth Doing. 240
Good Judgment 241
Longevity 242
What's He Worth? 243

Other Books by
Mitch Anthony 244

Acknowledgments

Thanks to my wife, Debbie, for the daily doses of love, encouragement, editing in the small things, strategy in the big things, and for the many great chapters we've written together.

Thank you, Nate, Nic, Sophia, and Alec, for the daily doses of play, time together, and the true meaning you've brought into my life.

Thank you, Dad, for being the force of optimism that has driven these messages to outposts they would never have seen.

Thank you, Greg Wimmer, for your art and artistic spirit.

Thank you, Cathie Armstrong, for your editorial labor of love.

Thank you, Joanna Chadwick, for your editing touches as well.

Thanks to all the radio station owners, managers, and program directors who have helped to bring these messages into the lives of so many people.

I owe all of you a great debt of gratitude.

Preface

In 1995, I brought a couple of pages, like those you will read in this book, to a local radio station and I made a recording. I asked the program director if he would like to have a regular feature called *The Daily Dose* each morning to give people a little "pick-me-up."

He surprised me by responding, "No, I'd like to air it every morning and *every evening* because people often need a 'pick-me-up' after work as well."

Little did I suspect where it would lead. Within a year, the feature was airing on more than 150 stations around the country. It seems that hardly a week goes by in my own town where someone will come to me and say, "I listen every day. Thank you for those words."

I am convinced that we are a nation of people who hunger for good news and positive views. Reports and evidence to the contrary abound, but in our souls we know that "Life is whatever we make it," which are the words with which I end every broadcast.

My prayer and hope is that these stories and ideas will help encourage you each day as you prepare to meet people and circumstances. If it works for you, I encourage you to pass this book on to others and help to shine the light of optimism in their lives as well.

If you would like these stories e-mailed to your workplace each week, you can do so by visiting *www.mitchanthony.com* and requesting the *Monday Morning Motivation* program.

It is common to meet the pessimist and the cynic. It is common to hear complaining, condemning, and criticizing. It is common to see people who have given up. We only live once, and we leave an impression wherever we go. Let us strive to be *uncommon*.

ATTITUDE

ADJUSTMENT

The Attitude Instrument

My first (and only) flight lesson was an event I will not soon forget. My instructor had a strange approach to teaching piloting skills. He would get you up to about 10,000 feet and then start hollering instructions. This teaching process tended to be a bit unnerving, especially on a first lesson.

Shortly into the flight he began to yell, "Look at your attitude."

I thought, "What? I feel good."

"No!" he was perturbed. "Look at your attitude!"

I looked at him incredulously wondering why he was doubting my mental approach.

He looked at me like I was an idiot, "Look at your attitude instrument."

"What's that?" I asked.

He pointed to an instrument that showed where the wings are in relationship to the horizon. It seemed my wings were a bit tilted. We were going to land, no doubt, but not on the wheels. He then showed me how to level my wings; or how to straighten out my attitude. When we reached ground, I realized that I had learned a good lesson from a poor teacher.

I had always believed that attitudes were about feelings and positive emotions – which I thought was just a put-on. After that flight lesson, I learned that attitude is nothing more than keeping yourself headed toward your stated goals; keeping your wings pointed to the horizon.

If the winds of adversity and discouragement blow you off course, do not give up. Rather, adjust and keep moving toward your goal. Attitude is not a feeling; it is a mental adjustment we must sometimes make a hundred times a day if we want to reach the horizon.

The Greatest Pitcher of All Time

The story is told about a young boy who went out into his yard to play baseball – all alone. This young fellow had big dreams. This was the week he would try out for a position on the local little league squad.

He picked up a bat and a ball and prepared himself. He announced, "Ladies and gentlemen, coming to bat is the greatest baseball player in the world."

He tossed the ball into the air, took a swing, and missed. "Strike one on the greatest baseball player in the world."

He tossed the ball a second time, took a mighty swing, and missed again. "Strike two on the greatest baseball player in the world."

With a look of dogged determination, he threw the ball one last time into the air, swung ferociously, and caught nothing but air. "Ladies and gentlemen," he announced, "the greatest baseball player in the world has just struck out to the greatest pitcher of all time."

Happiness Is Being Happy

We have so little time in this world to be happy, so we should not waste time on being unhappy.

A little girl once wrote to Carol Burnett, "Happiness is snuggling up in bed under all the blankets on a cold night. Happiness is just being happy." Now, that is a quote to remember.

It has been said that historian Will Durant looked for happiness in knowledge, and found disillusionment. He sought happiness in travel, and found weariness. He sought happiness in wealth, and found worry. He sought happiness in his writing, and found only fatigue.

One day he saw a woman waiting in a car with a sleeping baby in her arms. A man descended from a train and came over and gently kissed the woman and then the baby, ever so gently, so as not to awaken him. The family drove away leaving Durant with the sobering realization that "Every normal function of life holds some delight."

James Oppenheim said, "The foolish man seeks happiness in the distance; the wise man grows it under his feet."

The Ladder of Achievement

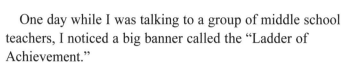

One day while I was talking to a group of middle school teachers, I noticed a big banner called the "Ladder of Achievement."

The ladder had ten steps that the students must climb figuratively with their attitudes in order to achieve anything of significance in their lives.

Before Step 1 - I won't.
Step 1 - I can't.
Step 2 - I don't know how.
Step 3 - I wish I could.
Step 4 - Asks, "What is it?"
Step 5 - I think I might.
Step 6 - I might.
Step 7 - I think I can.
Step 8 - I can.
Step 9 - I will.
Step 10 - I did.

I would venture to say that these ten steps are not just for school children. Many adults get their feet stuck on at least one rung on this ladder of attitude.

All good journeys and achievements start with a single attitudinal step.

Getting Started

They say it takes 80 percent of the fuel on board the space shuttle just to get it out of the earth's atmosphere, and it can cruise multiple times around the earth on the remaining 20 percent.

That is 80 percent of the total fuel supply just to get started!

One fellow told me he did not have a hard time believing this, as it took 80 percent of a pot of coffee just to get him out his front door.

Getting started is always the toughest part of any journey. The first step can be shaky. Our muscles ache, we struggle for balance, and our feet are sore. But we plod on, putting one foot ahead of the other. Pretty soon we get into a rhythm; and after awhile, it seems like we could go forever.

A psychological law applies here: "We create our own momentum." Others may cheer us on in the race, but we are the one that has to run. People cannot move our feet for us.

Today, instead of just thinking about it, go ahead and get something started. You may end up in a whole new atmosphere.

Ketchup

Three high-powered businessmen went out to do a power lunch. One of the businessmen ordered a steak burger with fries. When the fries came, he noticed that there was no ketchup and abruptly pulled over the busboy. "Bring me some ketchup!" he commanded.

The busboy nodded and walked away.

Ten minutes later, the man's fries were cold and he *still* had no ketchup. Doubly perturbed, he pulled the busboy over again and brusquely asked, "Didn't I ask you for the ketchup?"

"Yeah," the busboy answered.

"And you didn't bring it?" the businessman queried.

The busboy answered, "Nope."

"Maybe you don't know who I am," the businessman retorted.

The busboy asked, "Who are you?"

The businessman smugly answered, "I'm the number one employer in this town. I own many businesses. Chances are my businesses employ one or both of your parents. I, politically and economically, control this community. That's who I am."

The busboy did not seem all that impressed. "Well sir," he replied, "maybe you don't know who I am."

"Who, may I ask, are *you*?" asked the businessman.

The busboy replied, "I'm the one who's in charge of the ketchup."

To do a good job, people must feel they are important – even if it means being in charge of the ketchup.

I Could've Given More

In Steven Spielberg's award-winning film, *Schindler's List*, there is a dramatic and gripping scene at the end that speaks to every heart.

The Jews, whose lives are spared because of Oscar Schindler's efforts, are thanking him for what he has done. More than a thousand lived because of his mercy and courage (descendants of these 1,000+ people today outnumber all of the Jews currently living in Poland).

Rather than feeling proud of what had he done, Schindler was overcome by what he had not done. His car, had he sold it, could have paid for five more lives, and his watch could have saved another. From a stricken heart, he yells to those offering their gratitude, "I could've done more; I could've given more."

Who among us cannot relate to those profound words?

Each day we see opportunities to enrich the lives of others, better our communities, and brighten another person's day.

That which we keep to ourselves may give us limited satisfaction, but what we give away to others gives an enduring sense of purpose and joy.

I am beginning to understand more and more what my father meant when he said, "The only things you keep in this world are the things you give away."

Tragically Comic

Life and people are a strange mixture of comedy and tragedy. Some people I meet are comically tragic, and others are tragically comic.

I have found if you want to survive in this world, you must be able to laugh. Laugh easily, laugh often, and laugh at yourself.

One person said, "If you can laugh at it, you can live with it."

Or, as one mother so aptly stated, "Blessed are they who can laugh at themselves, they will never cease to be amused."

Another mother put it this way, "Laughing at your problems is like changing a baby's dirty diaper; while it doesn't permanently solve anything, it sure makes things more livable for awhile."

Yes, life is a mixed bag of comedy and tragedy. Those who know will tell you that if it was not for the comedy, they could not have stood up to the tragedy. Comedy has a way of smoothing out the rough roads before us.

Laugh easily and laugh often – your survival depends on it.

The Present

There are some speeches you never forget. A woman stood up and announced to a crowd that her doctors had told her the cancer was inoperable and, of course, incurable. They gave her, at best, six months to live.

She told the crowd that since that day, she has treated every day as precious – like a priceless gift – because, for all she knows, it could be her last. She said she'd been living every day that way since her doctors informed her of the end … more than 14 years ago.

It is amazing how having too much of something can make us take it for granted, and how not having enough can make us cherish it. Tell people they are running out of life, and suddenly every day is worth living to the fullest. They have discovered the magic of the here and now.

I saw a *Family Circus* cartoon that said it well. The little girl was explaining to her brother: "Yesterday is past, tomorrow isn't here, but today is a gift. That's why it's called the present."

Time for a Time Out!

A popular discipline many parents use with children today is the time out. If Johnny and Suzy get out of hand, or become frustrating, obnoxious, or otherwise, their parents put them in a quiet place for reflection and contemplation.

During a basketball game when things are getting out of hand, the coach calls a time out.

Someone suggested to me that adults miss the perfect opportunity several times every day for a much-needed time out – the red light! "Watch others and yourself at the stoplight," he noted. "People are tense, in a hurry, and ready to pound the horn if the person in front doesn't move at the first hint of green. We're hurrying from one appointment to the next in this game called achievement, and what we really need is an occasional time out."

Maybe we have been reading these traffic lights wrong all along. Maybe a yellow light does not mean, "Hurry up!" but instead, means, "Slow down." A red light does not have to mean "Sit and stew," it can mean, "Kick back and relax."

This is just what we need when the game of life is moving too fast. At the next red light, take a time out!

Accidental Tourists

We all enjoy going on a good vacation, traveling to exotic places, and being charmed by unusual sights and people. It is usually a time of wonder, amazement, and enjoyment. Anita Diamant wrote:

"A tourist is simply a person who is unashamed of being curious about the place he or she has landed in. Tourists are grateful - and charmed by - the kindness of writers and other strangers. And tourists try to do as much and to have as good a time as possible, because they know they're not going to be around long enough to take it all in."

I recently saw a bumper sticker on a truck that read, "I'm just a tourist on this planet." The attitude of a tourist, according to this writer, is a great attitude to have toward our daily journey in life.

Life is about being curious about the world around us, appreciating the services others perform, and doing as much as we can in the time that we have.

We would experience more wonder, excitement, and appreciation if we just stopped long enough to realize that we are just passing through!

Weigh-In

I hated to sound ignorant, but I had to know. I was watching a line of trucks at the truckstop go through the scales to the weigh-in. I understood that trucks had weight limits, but I was curious about the specifics.

The fellow at the counter was well informed on such matters. "The highway patrol is very strict on weight restrictions," he said. "If trucks are overloaded, it restricts maneuverability for the drivers, which could place them in peril if they needed to stop suddenly or turn quickly. It also places the rest of us out there at risk. If these trucks with too much baggage don't lighten up, it makes the road dangerous for all of us."

"Maybe," I thought to myself, "we need this sort of scale on the road of life."

How much time do we all spend trying to get out of the way of those who carry too much emotional baggage? If we are going in the wrong direction and have trouble stopping, our trailers might be overloaded.

Every psychological support system is designed to carry only so much weight. If there are problems maneuvering, it is probably time to weigh-in and lighten up.

The road of life would then be a better and safer place for all of us.

The "Kee-Ya"

The girl could not have weighed any more than 60 pounds soaking wet. She was in the middle of a public Tae Kwon Do demonstration and the instructor was holding a board in front of her that she would soon attempt to break.

Scores of people were watching, but she seemed oblivious to her audience. Others before her who were bigger and stronger had tried and failed.

The place fell silent and all eyes were upon her. She had eyes of steel. You could see her breathing, slowly and with measure. She looked like a volcano building, but with total control.

Suddenly, she lifted her hand, let out a sharp "Kee-ya!" and parted the board clearly in half. Applause erupted around her.

Later I asked her instructor what the "Kee-ya" noise is for.

"It is for focus," he said. "You let all your energy build and then release it with total focus. The 'Kee-ya' helps you to release."

Watching that girl that day taught me why so many of my own efforts had failed. I had not been focused enough.

If you want to break a barrier in your life badly enough, you do it by giving it all you've got and holding nothing back.

Private Courage

The greatest acts of courage often do not make the evening news. Pulling people out of the fire and rescuing drowning victims are heroic, no doubt, but the people who perform them usually say that they only did what anyone else in their place would have done.

What do they mean by that? They are saying that we all have an instinct for courage; that it is a natural, spiritual inclination when great and oppressive circumstances rise against us.

In his book, *Growing Strong in the Seasons of Life,* Chuck Swindoll wrote:

> *"Courage is not limited to the battlefield or the Indianapolis 500 or bravely catching a thief in your house. The real tests of courage are much deeper and much quieter. They are the inner tests, like remaining faithful when no one is looking, like enduring pain when the room is empty, like standing alone when you're misunderstood."*

Unless you are Superman, opportunities for public heroism are rare. Opportunities for displaying courage, however, are with us each day.

Asking, "Why?"

My wife, Debbie, was a widow at 21-years-old. She was married to her husband for three months when they discovered he had lung cancer. Three months later he was dead.

She picked herself up and moved on in life. She worked her way through college and earned two degrees. I asked her how she dealt with such a setback at so early an age.

Her answer, "I learned to quit asking questions that couldn't be answered."

"Such as?" I asked.

She went on, "I found the real dead-end in a tragedy is when you start asking, 'Why?' You can ask that question all you want, but you're not going to get an answer. Every time you ask 'why?' you're just wasting your time."

After she stopped asking the wrong questions, she began asking the right ones. "Where do I go from here? Whose help do I need? What changes do I need? What constructive things can I do with my life?"

Debbie unlocked a great truth from which we can all learn. Sometimes the answer to life's greatest difficulties is simply asking the right questions.

An "I Can't" Attitude

It is often said that you must possess an "I can" attitude to succeed. While I agree with that view, I think success is equally dependent – or maybe even more dependent – on an "I can't" attitude.

Let me explain.

I see in myself (as well as in others) a dangerous tendency to try to do everything myself. As no one can be a master of all, we end up sacrificing quality and limiting our success.

Instead of delegating the things we are not good at to abler and more qualified hands, we try to do it all ourselves. Oftentimes, we do this to save money; and, eventually, we pay the price.

What we need is a very *positive* "I can't" attitude. For example:

- "I can't do everything."
- "I can't be everywhere at once."
- "I can't solve all the world's problems."
- "I can't make it without a little help from others."

These attitudes help us to focus on our talents, and success usually follows. Yes, the key to success for some might just be learning the "I can't" attitude.

ATTITUDE ADJUSTMENT

Smile, if You Can

All seven-year-old Chelsey Thomas wanted for Christmas was to be able to smile. It was not going to take a new doll or toy to make her smile, but it would take two operations.

You see, Chelsey has a rare disorder called Moebius Syndrome, where the mouth sags because she was born without a key nerve in her face. This nerve transmits commands to facial muscles that control smiling, frowning, and pouting.

Chelsey had been born with a perpetually grumpy look on her face, and she was excited about the two-part surgical procedure that would give her a smile.

"She'll be able to smile for the first time," her mother said, "and that's something every parent waits for. Usually it happens in the first few weeks, but we've had to wait a bit longer."

Seven years to be exact. And what is a smile worth? The two steps of the operation will cost $70,000!

Chelsey knows it is worth every penny because, after all, who wants to be a person who cannot smile? The rest of us ought to smile just because we can.

If you can think of any reason to do so today, smile – it won't cost you a penny.

The Town that Wasn't

Thousands of people are in love with the town of Liberty Falls, even though it does not really exist – except, that is, in the mind of its founder, Ralph Gadiel.

Gadiel was 52 years old when his collectibles business went broke. He felt like a beaten old man until he read a college thesis his daughter wrote on the "self-fulfilling prophecy."

"It taught me that you set your own course in life," says Gadiel. "A positive attitude can conquer anything."

Newly inspired at 53, he launched a new collectibles company. He created a fictional mining town, called Liberty Falls, made of three-inch porcelain buildings.

Determined not to repeat his mistakes, he began to sell only to large department stores (and to only one store per city). He sells only from October to December, and releases only nine new buildings per year. Customers line up for hours to get a piece of Liberty Falls.

Ralph Gadiel has learned that the only thing standing between an old dog and a new trick is the right attitude and a willingness to learn!

Blind Optimism

Winston Churchill said, "For myself I am an optimist – it does not seem to do much good being anything else."

One Fortune 500 CEO stated, "I've never met a rich pessimist."

If you were to ask your average pessimists why they are pessimistic, they would no doubt give an endless litany of circumstances turned sour and details that turned disappointing.

If disappointment and negative circumstances are the basis for pessimism, then why are there not more pessimists? Each one of us has to deal with negative circumstances and disappointments.

"Things going wrong" is not a logically sound reason to become a pessimist. Everyone is given a choice during, and following, each event they face – the choice to find a solution; the choice to overcome; the choice to live with enthusiasm and hope; and the choice to be creative.

These mental choices are what we call optimism. It seems strange to me how some use the phrase "blind optimism," but never, "blind pessimism." For it is the pessimist who cannot see an answer; while the optimist, faced with similar circumstances, can see all kinds of possibilities.

Hidden Opportunities

Joseph Sugarman stated, "Each problem has hidden in it an opportunity so powerful that it literally dwarfs the problem."

The greatest success stories were created by people who recognized a problem and turned it into an opportunity. Problems are dead-ends only to those who stop thinking.

As children, we learned about an inventor who was having trouble hearing. Instead of succumbing to such adversity, he began working on a device that, today, few of us could imagine living without—the telephone.

Alexander Graham Bell said, "When one door closes, another opens. But, we often look so long and regretfully upon the closed door, we do not see the ones which open for us."

These wise and revealing words are from a man who did not spend a whole lot of time staring at closed doors.

If today you face a problem, and if you think your problem is big, remember that your problem is not nearly as big as the opportunity it is concealing.

ATTITUDE ADJUSTMENT

That Winning Ingredient

I recently had the privilege of flying home seated next to a professional hockey scout, who also had been a NHL coach.

I asked him the only question I could think of asking a scout, "What are you looking for?"

"Other than the obvious – speed, strength, and agility – there is one key winning ingredient that is hard to find," he answered. "And that ingredient is 'coach-ability.'"

Successful coaches know that individuals with skill alone will not guarantee a winning team. It is like a friend told me about his work place, "You can always tell a manager, but you can't tell him much!"

If we are willing to take constructive criticism and accept instruction – especially from the people that report to us – we are guaranteed to improve. No matter how competent we think we are, we can always find room for improvement.

Skill is important. But eventually, we will find ourselves on a level playing field. At that point, becoming a champion will hinge on one winning ingredient – coach-ability!

The Moody Blues

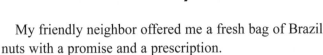

My friendly neighbor offered me a fresh bag of Brazil nuts with a promise and a prescription.

"These will make you happy," she promised. "They have selenium, which is proven to fight off depression. Just eat one or two a day."

People search in the strangest places for a guarantee of happiness. They want a way to control their moods, because they know that the ability to control their moods plays a huge role in their successes.

If Behavioral Science has taught us anything, it has taught us this: "Most people's moods can be altered by their actions."

However, most wait for the "right mood" to kick in before doing anything. They are missing the point; the action precipitates the emotion.

A bad mood, sluggish feeling, or depressed emotion can often be altered by exercising, getting organized, or doing something charitable for someone else.

These are the paths to choose to steer clear of the blues. And, I suppose, a Brazil nut can't hurt. It is better to eat nuts than to go nuts!

The H–A–L–T Rule

A man, who had successfully completed alcoholism treatment through Alcoholics Anonymous, told me, "A lot of guidelines they give to folks who have gone through life drunk would work just as well for sober folks."

He offered this example: "We were taught the H–A–L–T Rule when it came to dealing with anger and frustration. The wrong time to say or do anything is when you are:

H - Hungry
A - Angry
L - Lonely
T - Tired"

When you are ready to spout off and get yourself into deep or hot water, first ask yourself, "Am I hungry right now? Am I feeling lonely? Am I angry with someone? Or, am I just really tired?" For it is at these times that we are most susceptible and vulnerable to an emotional overload.

It is amazing how, after a good meal or a good night's sleep, the urge to spout off passes and our emotions settle.

Think about the H–A–L–T Rule the next time your mouth is tempted to run!

Dog Eat Dog

Man is supposedly the Supreme Being on this planet –
the highest form of animal life. At times, however, we could
learn from watching the behavior of the lesser beings with
whom we shares this planet.

Humorist Dave Barry made an adroit comparison
between horses and dogs on the topic of gratitude. He
wrote:

> *"You give a dog something totally wretched to eat,
> such as a wad of pre-chewed Dentyne gum, and the dog
> will henceforth view you as the Supreme Being. It will
> gaze on you for hours with rapt adoration and lick the
> ground you walk on and try to kill the pizza-delivery
> person if he comes anywhere near you.*
>
> *Whereas if you spend hours grooming a horse and
> lugging its food and water around, the horse will be
> thinking, 'Should I chomp on this person's arms?'"*

Even in the lower species we sincerely appreciate the
virtue of gratitude. It seems that, in a dog-eat-dog world,
the best we could do is be more like a dog!

When is Enough, Enough?

ATTITUDE ADJUSTMENT

Maybe you have met an individual like this: the parsimonious, old curmudgeon who watched every penny and never spent a dime; who enjoyed gathering, but never enjoyed the bounty he had gathered. About this type of individual, Bernard Baruch wrote:

"There is not much difference, really, between the squirrel laying up nuts and the man laying up money. Like the squirrel, the man – at least at the start – is trying to provide for his basic needs. I don't know much about the squirrels, but I think they know when they have enough nuts. In this way they are superior to men, who often don't know when they have enough, and frequently gamble away what they have in the empty hope of getting more."

So, when is enough, enough? When we can no longer enjoy what we've gathered and can only focus on gathering.

It is kind of like the bumper sticker you see on RVs rolling down the highway, "We're spending our children's inheritance."

They have already done their gathering; now, it is time to enjoy what they have gathered.

What You Say to Yourself

As children, most of us were taught the famous story by Wally Piper, *The Little Engine that Could!* The dolls and toys begged the little engine to try his hardest and to get them over the mountain. He began to say to himself, "I think I can! I think I can!" and inspired himself to make the journey.

Performance experts tell us that we are in danger of not reaching our potential if we forget the importance of how we talk to ourselves. Glenville Kleiser wrote:

> *"Just as you are unconsciously influenced by outside advertisements, so you can vitally influence your life from within by auto suggestion. The first thing each morning and the last thing each night, suggest to yourself specific ideas that you wish to embody in your character and personality. Address such suggestions to yourself, silently or aloud, until they are deeply impressed upon your mind."*

Most people practice self-talk, but too often the talk is negative. The words we whisper to ourselves should be complimentary, positive, and uplifting – instead of degrading and condemning.

Most people understand the importance of the words we speak. The most important words, however, are those we speak to ourselves.

Comfort Zones

Try this little experiment:

Fold your hands in front of you. Notice which thumb is on top – left or right. Now, refold your hands so the other thumb ends up on top. This probably feels awkward, strange, uncomfortable – even weird or "wrong."

Notice what your body wants to do. It wants go back to the original position – or what it considers a normal position. Let your thumb go back to that position. How does that feel? You are once again feeling comfortable and at ease.

This little thumb exercise illustrates why most people never attain their desired level of living – they fear the discomfort of going out of their comfort zones.

Stan Dale said, "Comfort zones are plush, lined coffins. When you stay in your plush, lined coffin you die."

Growth, development, and advancement require a certain degree of discomfort. People rarely feel instantly at ease with new and unfamiliar approaches to life and work.

People who continue to grow and succeed have learned to be comfortable with the uncomfortable!

Wisest of the Athenians

Who was the wisest of the Athenians? The ancient Athenian culture was one that prided itself on its ability to think and develop sound logic. It produced classic thinkers such as Socrates, Aristotle, and Demosthenes.

One day, Socrates broke strides with his wise reputation by announcing, "I am the wisest of the Athenians."

People were shocked. This man's reputation was one of thoughtfulness and humility, never arrogance or pomposity. They demanded that he justify his claim.

Socrates explained himself this way, "Today so many Athenians claim to know all there is to know about every mystery. This convinces me that I am the wisest Athenian of all because I *know* that I do *not know*; therefore, I must be the wisest."

How many people do you know who have been fooled into thinking they are really smart? They think their expertise in one realm carries over into all areas of life; therefore, they have an answer for everything.

If you wish to be the "wisest," follow Socrates' lead and achieve it by asking the right questions – instead of trying to provide all the answers.

ATTITUDE ADJUSTMENT

Constant Cultivation

Have you ever left home for a week or two and come back only to find your lawn and garden taken over by "The Invasion of the Mutant Weed?"

You left. The rain came. The weeds grew. You pulled them. You killed them. They came back. No matter what you try, they always seem to find a way back. How quickly weeds come, and how quickly they grow.

Our lives and thoughts – like our lawns and gardens – require constant cultivation. Once is simply not enough. The fact that you made a good decision to have a good attitude a month ago just will not cut it. Quit paying attention to your attitude for a week or two, and behold the weeds that have staked a claim.

King Solomon wrote thousands of years ago, "I looked on my garden and received instruction, it was overgrown with thorns and it's wall was broken down."

This great king looked at his garden and learned about life. There are many lessons there. The next time you tend your lawn or garden, take a long look and *think.*

Oh, and by the way, don't forget to pick those dandelions — I don't want them blowing over into my yard.

The Greatest Power

In the Steven Spielberg movie, *Schindler's List*, we are given one of the most poignant portraits of what real human power is.

In the film, Schindler is trying to dissuade a drunken, bloodthirsty, hate-mongering German officer from killing another Jew over a minor infraction.

This officer had a reputation for killing over the slightest offense, and sometimes just for the sport of it. This officer is not only drunken with liquor but drunken with power as well.

He is about to kill a child when Schindler plays to his ego: "Show them the power you have. Not by killing, but by releasing him. They expect you to kill. The ultimate power is the power to free."

The officer liberated the boy.

This scene is a dramatic illustration of how humans can pollute the concept of power. True power is not having a chokehold on others to control them; rather, it is having control of ourselves and using that power to love and help those around us.

E. H. Chapin wrote, "I am never more strong than when I forego revenge and dare to forgive."

Continuous Improvement

Tom Peters, the best-selling author and business visionary, once said, "Excellent firms don't believe in excellence - only in constant improvement and constant change."

Great people act and think like great businesses. In fact, people that think this way are the reason we have great businesses, schools, churches, and organizations.

The groups and the people that always trail in the race of progress are those who are heard saying things like, "We've always done it this way," or "We tried that once before," or "Why change? Things are OK as they are."

I have an acid test to determine whether or not an individual or a group will be successful. I begin by asking the simple question, "Are you successful?"

If people start telling me how great they are and inflate all they have done, I know they are in the "down curve" of success.

If they answer something like, "I could always do better," or " I'm improving," or "I don't feel like I've scratched the surface yet," then I know they are still on their way up!

Improvement is not something that just happens, but a state of mind that is always happening.

Words – The Attitude Food

We are a society that believes in nourishing our bodies. Some of us, however, nourish our bodies like we are heading into hibernation.

When our stomachs send even the slightest hunger signal, we respond. We want food and we want it now! Our world is now full of fast-food restaurants. But fast food wasn't fast enough, so we invented the drive-thru.

We eat to keep up our energy. If only we treated our mind and emotions with the same care and immediacy that we treat our own bodies. Words are the nourishment for our minds and emotions. Throughout the day, our minds send out constant hunger pangs such as:

- Frustration
- A pessimistic or negative outlook
- Anger at every little thing that goes wrong

The fact that we ate a good meal last week does not carry us over to today. Neither can we be motivated and directed today, by some good words we read a week ago.

A hunger for knowledge and good words is key to keeping our energy life high. And, remember, the only knowledge that really matters is what you learn – *after* you know it all!

Childlike Wonder

An inventor was sitting in a park, watching children extract extreme pleasure from playfully wrestling in the sand – and the "Tickle Me Elmo" was born in his mind.

Recently, in my home I had to replace a light bulb on a 15-foot ceiling. Since I had no ladder (and no intention of buying one), I was trying to figure how to reach the light fixture.

One of my children suggested, "You don't need to climb up; let's make a long arm and a hand."

I watched in awe as my children found a long pole and attached their homemade "hand," made from an old kitchen utensil and finely-sculpted masking tape.

We raised the "arm" and "hand" and voila! – the light bulb adhered and came out. We then replaced the new bulb the same way.

The "Tickle Me Elmo" and our homemade "hand" and "arm" stories illustrate the same truth: life is better, easier, and more fun – when lived with childlike wonder.

A capacity for childlike wonder carried into adult life typifies both the creative and the fulfilled person. Kids like adventurous challenges. They do not look at a challenge as "another stinking problem" – until adults teach them to do so.

A simple key for living a wonderful adulthood is: Never lose your sense of childlike wonder.

"Good Shot, Daddy!"

My wife and I decided to play a round of golf and take our young children along with us.

On the first hole, I had a slippery downhill putt from about 15 feet, and I just hammered it – 25 feet past the hole! I was mad at myself for my lack of finesse.

"What a way to start my round," I thought. "Go from a potential birdie to a bogey, maybe worse."

My pessimism, however, was interrupted by my children's enthusiastic responses to my poor putt.

"Good shot, Daddy!" my four-year-old daughter yelled with glee.

"Yeah, Daddy, good shot!" piped up my two-year-old son.

They were just ecstatic!

My wife and I looked at each other and burst out laughing. Our children understood the purpose of being on the golf course better than we did. We should have been out there just having fun and not letting any circumstances spoil our time together.

Their exuberant laughter relaxed me and their ignorant, blissful attitudes re-focused me. So I walked up to that 25-foot uphill putt and knocked it into the middle of the cup.

Now when I hit an errant shot in life, I can hear my children's echo, "Good shot, Daddy!"

The CLOs

Failure is a much better teacher than success – a lesson many corporations are learning.

When things are going well, we tend to put our lives into cruise control. Some of us even take our hands off the wheel, or stop watching the road altogether.

Most corporations – and individuals – fail to learn from their failures. It has been said that if we fail to learn, we learn to fail.

Many large companies like Coca-Cola, Monsanto, and Hewlett-Packard have hired CLOs (Corporate Learning Officers) to make sure their organizations are using information productively. Corporations need CLOs to help their employees analyze failures, which in turn helps them avoid repeating the same mistakes.

Likewise in a marriage, if both spouses studiously analyzed and learned from mistakes, we would see stronger bonds – and fewer broken ones.

We learn to fail when we fail to learn. Our purpose is not to succeed – it is to learn. When we learn, we cannot help but succeed.

Three-Part Cure

One of the best books I have ever read is *Anatomy of an Illness* by Norman Cousins.

Cousins, a writer and editor who often wrote on health issues, was diagnosed as having an incurable disease that doctors said would eventually debilitate and kill him.

Cousins wasted no time and, immediately, designed his own program for healing based on his years of observation in the world of Health Science.

First, he made sure his own doctor would nourish his will to live. He made it clear that he did not need pessimism and skepticism – which would only zap his spirit. Cousins had observed many patients who gave up the will to fight based solely on doctors' attitudes.

Second, he began taking mega-doses of Vitamin C – up to ten grams a day.

Third, he dedicated at least 30 to 60 minutes per day to laugh. He watched comedies and read funny stories.

Cousins' program worked. The incurable disease left his body. Thirty years later he was teaching his ideas at UCLA's medical school.

Nourish the will to live; get nutrition and laugh – a simple three-part cure from Norman Cousins.

Work for Play

Edmond Boreaux Szekely wrote, "The majority work to make a living: some work to acquire wealth or fame, while a few work because there is something within them which demands expression, only a few truly love it."

When we examine people at work, we find attitudes and values that seem to contradict much of what our western culture holds as normal. We are cautioned not to work too much or too hard.

Work for many people has become a compartmentalized facet of their lives. Fun does not seem to fit into the same compartment. People speak of "blue" Monday, "hump-day" Wednesday, and then exult, "Thank God, it's Friday!"

These statements only demonstrate that, to many, the workweek is filled with drudgery and thankless toil.

The most fulfilled people, however, are those who have found expression through their work. They have turned their work into an opportunity to release their creativity and energy. When work ceases to feel like work, it is no longer work.

What is the perfect job? People talk about more pay, while others talk about more "play." Are you engaged in work that allows you to collect a "play-check?"

For, Not Against

There was once a training film entitled, *The Man in the Mirror,* about Fred, a middle manager in his 40s. Fred had come to the point where security was about the only thing that mattered to him. He had no real vision, passion, or focus for the future. He had become obsolete – and did not know it.

One day while he was sitting at home, his teenage son walked in and asked, "Dad, I'm curious, what are you for?"

"Son, that's a good question," Fred responded. "But, first let me tell some things you better be looking out for with some of your friends and the crowd at school."

He began to deliver a monologue about all the things he was against.

His son's face slowly dropped and he nervously excused himself saying, "Uh, gee, Dad, thanks, I've gotta run now."

Fred had dampened his son's philosophical curiosity by being cynical and skeptical. His son wanted to know what he was for, and found out that he was for himself and against everything else.

People are drawn to those who are passionate. No matter what we oppose, we must offer a solution, an answer, or an alternative.

People who are for something often find that people are for them.

Rich with Happiness

"If you're seeking an improved existence this year, keep in mind that happiness is in no way connected to wealth." These are the words of economic historian and author, Richard Easterlin.

Easterlin has found that, although the gross domestic product per capita in the United States has more than doubled in the last half century, there has been absolutely no improvement in the percentage of happy people.

"Even though each generation has more income than its predecessor, each generation wants more than its predecessor," points out Easterlin.

He states that one of our most enduring cultural beliefs is that another 10 to 20 percent increase in income would make each one of us perfectly happy. The flaw in that belief is that it does not take into account that aspirations rise as incomes rise.

In other words, by the time they finally get what they want, they will probably want something else. If today they are trying to keep up with the Jones', they could eventually find themselves trying to keep up with the Bill Gates' of the world.

True happiness lies in wanting what we have, not in what we do not have.

Fired Up or Burned Out

What is the difference between being "fired up" and being "burned out" with the work you do?

According to a Professional Work Force Survey by Peter McLaughlin Co., it could be one simple thing: whether or not you possess a good sense of humor.

According to this survey, a sense of humor helps on the job in three specific ways:

1. People with a sense of humor are three times as likely to report top levels of energy than those who don't have a sense of humor.
2. Ninety percent of respondents believe that a sense of humor helps them to perform better at work.
3. People with a sense of humor are half as likely to get anxious or frustrated in fixing problems and are twice as likely to be able to pull themselves out of bad moods.

A ready wit holds some powerful personal keys to success. People who laugh often do not run out of fuel as quickly as the "dead serious." People who can laugh at their mistakes are quicker to correct them and, therefore, perform better. People who laugh easily are in better control of their moods and attitudes.

A key to staying "fired up" is to laugh easily — and laugh often.

Mind Your Body

This is not your average, everyday grandpa. No, sir. Every day of the week, Mr. B. goes to the health club with his teenage grandson and works out on weights and spends an hour on the treadmill. Grandpa, by the way, is 72.

He believes that by taking care of your body, you end up taking care of your mind. "A sluggish body eventually leads to a lethargic mind," he told me. "When your body is in shape, your mind stays sharp, quick, and alert."

If you are willing to let your house go to waste, it is just a matter of time before you stop caring for the inhabitant as well.

I recently saw a study by a gerontologist who started people in retirement homes on daily weight-lifting programs. Without exception, the participants' strength and energy levels increased, along with their vitality and zest for living. The youngest person in the study was 84 – the oldest was 96.

How we treat our bodies is often a reflection of how much regard we have for our mind's potential and inner abilities.

We hear much talk about the mind-body connection, and I think it starts with the body. If you want to improve your state of mind, you can start by minding your body!

Know What You Are Good At

Author Richard Carlson writes about what his father used to say when reading his poorly written essays: "Richard, it's not important that you're not a great speller. It's really important, however, that you know that you're not a good speller. That way, when in doubt, you can use the dictionary."

Carlson's father was right – and not just about spelling. The same rule can be applied to virtually every aspect of our lives.

It is important for each of us to face the skills at which we are deficient. Adopting an attitude of humility and coach-ability will go a long way toward getting help and improving our performances.

I once went to a job interview and handed over my resume that listed my weaknesses first! They told me they had never seen a resume like that before.

And, I got the job.

People are impressed with those who are not afraid to admit and deal with their shortcomings. Just as important as it is to believe in yourself, it is equally important to know when to doubt yourself.

More Than Two Sides

According to Deborah Tannen, author of *The Argument Culture: Moving From Debate to Dialogue*, we have become a nation of arguers.

Tannen contends that a big piece of this argumentative puzzle is our use of metaphors in speech and in the media. Headlines scream about wars and battles – not just when describing real wars, but everyday conflicts between people and political parties. The argument culture has become so pervasive that many now take the attitude to the road, and the result is road rage.

To overcome our American habit of seeing every issue in absolutes, Tannen advises that we expand our notion of debate to include more dialogue.

To accomplish this, we must make a special effort not to think in twos. Most debates in our society assume there are two sides to every issue – no more, no less. This assumption has led to such insanity as hearing out the view that the Holocaust never happened.

Instead of asking, "What is the other side?," begin asking, "What are the other sides?" Instead of hearing both sides, begin looking for all sides.

If it is truth we seek, we will be quick to recognize that there may be more than two sides to every argument.

What Money Cannot Buy

I once read a quote that said, "Money can't buy happiness but it will purchase its accessories." Author Arne Garborg poses an interesting argument about what money cannot buy:

> *"It is said that for money you can have everything, but you cannot. You can buy food, but not appetite; Medicine, but not health; Knowledge, but not wisdom; Glitter, but not beauty; Fun, but not joy; Acquaintances, but not friends; Servants but not faithfulness; Leisure, but not peace. You can have the husk of everything but not the kernel!"*

What powerful words those are! Material wealth only gives the opportunity to buy the appearance of the trappings of happiness.

All of us possess some "kernels" if we look deep enough. Contented lives come from obtaining that which money cannot buy.

ATTITUDE ADJUSTMENT

At Your Own Expense

What is healthy humor? I have long been a proponent of an active sense of humor being a key to lowering stress, dissolving tension, and providing a healthier view of life. But, where does humor cross the line and become unhealthy? *When it is at another person's expense.*

To prevent this from happening, the best thing we can do is learn to laugh at ourselves, especially if we have a tendency to wear our feelings on our sleeves.

The healthiest people I know – from a psychological point of view – are those who are in touch with their shortcomings and weaknesses, and can laugh at their mistakes and foolishness.

Ben Franklin wryly wrote, "Who is wise? He that learns from everyone. Who is powerful? He who governs his passion. Who is rich? He that is content. Who is that? Nobody!"

Franklin recognized his own weaknesses and could laugh about it.

One nice thing about being able to laugh at yourself is that you will never run out of comedy material!

Ending the Guilt Trip

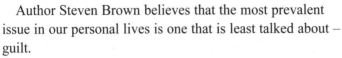

Author Steven Brown believes that the most prevalent issue in our personal lives is one that is least talked about – guilt.

In his Psychology training at Harvard, Brown discovered that almost every emotional illness includes a significant degree of guilt, for the tentacles of guilt go deep and wide:

- *Guilt separates us from others.* Most of us in our lifetime will only have a few close friends (A close friend is someone who knows almost everything about you – and is still your friend).
- *Guilt is what makes us judgmental and critical toward others.* Most folks throw up a smoke screen of criticism. They figure that if they can divert attention away from themselves, they won't have to face their own guilt.

Most people believe that when they feel guilt, they should stop doing the things that make them feel guilty. Quite the opposite is true; guilt drives people deeper into self-destructive behavior.

How, then, do we address guilt? The answer is with forgiveness. First, talk to a pastor, rabbi, priest, or spiritual counselor to find forgiveness and the roots of personal guilt. Second, seek forgiveness from those you know you have hurt. The final step is to begin forgiving yourself; you are human.

The journey of life was never meant to be a guilt trip.

ATTITUDE ADJUSTMENT

The Happiness Paradox

Dr. Victor Frankl, Auschwitz survivor and author of the classic, *Man's Search for Meaning,* once wrote: "To the degree you pursue happiness, to that same degree happiness will elude you."

This is known as the happiness paradox. When you spend your efforts, resources, and energy on achieving happiness, it eludes your grasp. When you resign yourself to the subtler joys and pleasures of life, happiness abounds. Many people struggle with this paradox.

Schopenhauer wrote, "Man is never happy, but spends his whole life in striving after something he thinks will make him so."

Lord Byron said, "There comes forever something between us and what we deem our happiness."

Robert Burns wrote, "If happiness has not seat and center in the breast, you may be wise or rich or great, but never can be blessed."

The happy person is the one who responds with tranquillity, joy, and hope in all circumstances.

And, Dr. Frankl's prescription for happiness? "Happiness is a by-product of giving yourself to something larger than yourself, of giving yourself to another in love."

Working At Humor

Joel Goodman, Director of the Humor Project, thinks we seriously need to take a new look at humor in the workplace.

Goodman, who holds a Doctorate in Education, teaches how humor can be used to make everything, from businesses to hospitals, run better.

Too many workplaces are over-serious because they have misconceptions about humor at work. "Humor does not equal joke telling or goofing off in front of the customer," Goodman said. "We need to reach our goals, but at the same time, we don't have to take ourselves so seriously."

But, what about the bottom line?

To answer that question, Goodman points to the example set by Southwest Airlines. They encourage employees to have fun at work and have a sense of humor. Southwest Airlines, one of the highest rated airlines for customer satisfaction, enjoyed a stretch of being in the black for over 25 years – a rare achievement in the airline industry.

"They make lots of money but have lots of fun," Goodman said. "They do not hire someone without a sense of humor."

When employees feel free to loosen up around their managers or colleagues, their stress levels go down and that translates into healthier employees. Also, it is a proven fact that a more relaxed atmosphere lends to more creativity which, ultimately, leads to an enduring business.

For those who wish to survive in today's business climate, humor is a critical part of serious business.

Stay Until You Like It

How do you get to the place where you can enjoy your work? If you listen to Milton Garland, the key is, "Get into something and stay with it until you like it."

Garland should know – he is 102 years old and the nation's oldest worker. He has been on the same job for 78 years!

"I love the work I'm doing," Garland said. "My advice is to go into something and stay with it until you like it. You can't like it until you obtain expertise in that work. Once you are an expert, it is a pleasure. And once you like what you do, you don't want to quit doing it."

Garland is an expert in what he does. He holds 40 patents, most involving innovations in refrigeration technology. He went to work for the Frick Company of Waynesboro, Pennsylvania, in the early 1920s, rising to Vice President of Education. He currently works 20 hours a week.

When asked, "Where would you be if you had retired 37 years ago at age 65?" Garland answered, "I'd be in my grave."

He is one of many in our nation who believes that retirement is a great, unchecked killer.

Garland's attitudes have helped his longevity. He never worries. He believes every problem has a solution. He thinks common sense will handle most difficulties (by the way, he eats most anything except sauerkraut).

His on-the-job pointers are, "Dig your heels into your work, keep learning, and stick with it until you like it."

"Can-Do" Attitudes

Do you have a "can-do" attitude? Throw an idea out on the table and watch people respond. Individuals start moving to one polarity or another. Either we can do this, or we cannot do this. The rest of what they say will be rationalization for one of these attitudinal polarities.

Let's compare the "can't-do" and "can-do" mindsets.

The "can't-do's" say: "We've never done it before. It's too complicated. We don't have the resources. There's not enough time. We already tried it. We don't have the expertise. It's good enough as it is."

The "can-do's" say: "We have the opportunity to be first. Look at it from a different angle. Necessity is the mother of invention. We'll re-evaluate some priorities. We learned from the experience. We will network with those who do. We can always make it better."

Contrasts of "can't-do" and "can-do" mentalities can go on ad infinitum. Our own attitudes can sway between these two extremes from day to day, depending on our moods and physical and mental states.

"Can't-do" attitudes lead to frustration, cynicism, bitterness, and burn out.

"Can-do" attitudes require more vigilance and persistence, but lead to greater optimism, hope, inner satisfaction.

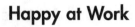

Happy at Work

Janet could not remember the last time she woke up feeling this happy. It had been about as many years as she had been in this job. Thirteen work days ago, Janet had given her two-week notice. After almost a decade of miserable employment, she was quitting and today was her last day!

She woke up with the most enthusiasm and happiest state-of-mind she had ever experienced. For the first time she was going to work happy because it was her last day of work – or, so she thought.

A funny thing happened on that last day of work. Janet walked through the front doors smiling. She greeted everyone cheerily and they all seemed different today. They all smiled at her cheerfulness and warmed up to her. They seemed to like her today.

Halfway through the day it dawned upon her: she had created her own unhappiness in this job. People smiled today because she smiled first. They were happy to see her because she acted happy to see them. Janet decided her work was not finished. She decided then and there to keep her job.

It has been 12 years since Janet decided to quit her job. Instead, she simply decided to quit coming to work with a sour attitude!

No Whiners Allowed

Have you ever noticed that successful people spend very little time whining and complaining about adverse circumstances? This is true even though they have overcome many challenging circumstances to get where they are.

On the other hand, nothing is more common than hearing struggling individuals whining, complaining, and condemning. Their energy is directed at fixing the blame instead of fixing the problem.

Abe Lincoln said, "Any fool can complain, condemn and criticize and...most fools do."

The only question we need to try to answer is this: "What comes first, the success or the attitude?"

The correct answer is, the "whine not" attitude that precedes success. Those who have learned not to whine have also learned the magic of asking, "Why not?" or "Why not me?" or "Why not now?"

If you desire success, remember that the door to this exclusive club reads, "No Whiners Allowed."

New Tricks for Old Dogs

They say you can't teach an old dog new tricks. That might be true, but have they ever wondered whether an old dog could teach us some new tricks?

I recently read a story about a dog owner that invested in the latest dog restraint technology – the invisible fence. It works like this: You install an electric antenna. You then place a battery-operated shocker on the dog's neck. If the dog tries to cross the invisible fence – zap! He gets a lesson he will not soon forget.

It sure sounds like a space-age solution, but it did not work for at least one dog owner. You see, his dog figured out that if he got close to the border – but not on it – it would set off a slight zap in the collar that wasn't enough to cause any serious discomfort. His dog kept repeating this action until he wore the battery down and then walked right out of the yard!

That old dog has some tricks to teach. If you've got patience, you can put up with a little discomfort. And, if you know where you want to go, you can overcome just about anything.

Resilience

The psychological catchword of the New Millennium just might be "resilience" – the ability to get through, get over, and thrive after trauma, trials, and tribulations.

According to author Frema Walsh, "Because our lives are so constantly under stress, because change is everywhere, we realize we can't look for calm waters anymore. Resilience means we can be challenged and not break down."

Many studies have been conducted to find out why some teams and athletes perform better after defeat, and why some cancer patients survive the worst possible odds.

Resilience comes more naturally to some, but it can be learned. Pediatric expert Michael Resnick says, "Some come into the world with a physical hardiness and calmness as opposed to easy excitability or irritability."

Resnick believes that resilience means going back toward your childlike nature – curiosity and questioning, playfulness, innate morality, and nobility.

One key to resilience is what Dr. Al Seibert, author of *The Survivor Personality,* calls "the learning reaction." He states:

"The people who are most resilient have a learning reaction, not a victim reaction, to bad events. It's distressing, they don't like it, but the question is, 'Do they have a learning/coping reaction or a victim/blaming reaction?' With all the downsizing and uncertainty in our world, people have to become more self-reliant and flexible - more resilient - than ever in modern history."

It is impossible to go through life without getting bounced around. The big question is whether or not we know how to bounce back.

The Human Frog

In the *Great Little Book of Sports,* we read about Raymond Enry, of the United States, who won more Olympic gold medals than any other athlete in history – more than Mark Spitz and Carl Lewis.

As a child, Raymond Enry was an invalid and confined to a wheelchair. One day a doctor suggested that Raymond start an exercise program to strengthen his legs. Ray, never a quitter, was determined to walk under his own power some day. He began to invent exercises of his own. After years of hard work, Ray performed the impossible – he walked by himself!

But that wasn't enough for Ray. He continued a vigorous exercise program that gave him superhuman springing abilities that amazed coaches as he began to compete in track. He was given the nickname, "The Human Frog."

In 1900, at the age of 27, Ray competed in the Olympics and won three gold medals. In 1904, he won three more in jumping events. In 1906 and 1908, he won a total of four – for a grand total of ten gold medals!

Raymond Enry's leap into the record books from the wheelchair proves, once again, that there is no greater power than a mind made up.

Power of Passion

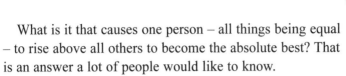

What is it that causes one person – all things being equal – to rise above all others to become the absolute best? That is an answer a lot of people would like to know.

A Dutch psychologist wanted to figure out what separated chess masters from chess grand masters. He subjected a group of each level to a battery of tests - I.Q., memory and spatial reasoning. He found absolutely no testing difference between them. The only difference he could find was that the Grand Chess Masters simply loved chess more! They had superior passion and commitment to the game.

Could passion be the key that leads to superior performance? Passion seems to unlock many powerful mechanisms of the mind:

- An optimism that searches for possibilities.
- A determination that won't take "no" for an answer.
- A creative outlook that revels in innovation and new strategies.
- A sense of purpose that burns brightly even when circumstances impart a bleak picture.

Take special note of the passion level of individuals who have risen highest in their fields. This passion, more likely than not, is what brought them to this place.

An enthusiastic love for life, along with an unquenchable thirst for betterment, is what passion is all about.

Rolling the Dice

Is there a way to take the risk out of living? If so, would such a life be worth living?

I was intrigued as I walked through a casino and watched the eagerness and enthusiasm with which people threw away their money.

Then the thought struck me, "Gambling is nothing more than misguided optimism! The attitude is great, but the application leaves something to be desired."

Gamblers wake up every day believing, "This will be my lucky day!" They return again and again to the green felt tables and racetracks with wide-eyed optimism. They know that you win some and you lose some.

While we could all do without the waywardness and impulsiveness of the gambler's psyche, we could all benefit from a renewed daily optimism as we approach this game called life.

Do we wake up expecting to win or lose? Do we put yesterday's losses behind us? Do we step up to the line and throw the dice, or do we hide when faced with risk?

Life is a gamble. Each venture into a relationship or opportunity is a risk. But in the game of life, the odds of success are with you when you are willing to take a chance.

You can bet on it!

Heading North

Nothing could have been worse news for a young athlete. His doctor had rendered the verdict, "You cannot play baseball, football, or participate in any other athletic events."

Temptation eventually got a hold of this kid, as each day he had to drive past a golf course. "Maybe, I could do that," he thought.

So, he told his doctor about his idea to try golf.

His doctor rebutted, "You can't play golf on crutches!"

But this kid was persistent. He rode a cart, hobbled to his ball, laid down his crutches, and hit the ball. Day after day he repeated this routine until he began to notice his legs gaining strength.

Eventually, this young man shed both the cart and his crutches. This persistent spirit and unyielding optimism eventually lead Andy North to an U.S. Open Championship and a bright, professional career.

Those of us who wish to head "north" on the ladder of accomplishment would do well to exercise such persistence and brightness of spirit.

In the words of Robert Louis Stevenson, "Keep your fears for yourself, but share your courage with others."

Soul of the Job

"Most of us have jobs that are too small for our spirits." This statement was made by Studs Terkel, recorder of *The American Voice.*

In the last couple of years, perhaps because of job security fears and wage stagnation, more workers are searching for the soul of their jobs.

Before we dismiss Terkel's observation as "New Age psycho-babble," we must recognize that people are trying to discover meaning in their jobs. They are looking for identity and self-worth amid mergers, job cuts, and numbers crunching. People are looking for a set of principles that are behaved at work. They want their work to mean something, and desire a higher level of trust in their workplace.

For a job to have meaning, there must be an opportunity for employees to express their creativity, inspiration, and ideas for innovation. To feel good about their work, people need to feel that what they do in some way helps those around them.

In the end, it is not one, sole job that provides fulfillment, but a job with soul!

Sure Beats Walking

On a recent flight, I was amazed at the conduct of a passenger who felt he had been slighted. Apparently, the man thought he was supposed to be seated in first class and it was overbooked.

Brushing his dignity and humor aside, he ranted and raved throughout the entire flight. He had missed out on his soft seat and cocktails and, by gosh, somebody was going to pay!

How easily we get spoiled. How quickly we lose perspective and forfeit gratitude over the conveniences we possess.

I thought about how nice it was to be able to fly two hours instead of driving 15 hours. Yet that 15-hour drive looks awfully good to the person on the 24-hour bus ride. And that bus ride looks luxurious to the person standing on the road with a thumb in the air. A hundred years ago, the same trip took two weeks.

We have it quite good in this modern world. Hopefully, we won't throw a tantrum over a temporary loss of luxury.

No matter how we get to where we are going, it sure beats walking!

BUILDING
RELATIONSHIPS

Things Aren't So Bad

Many people are afraid of intimate relationships because of all the morbid statistics they hear. But, are all these statistics true? According to Daniel Lynch, they are not. He writes:

"How many times have you heard or read that 50 percent of U.S. marriages end in divorce. It is not true. Yes, the number of divorces each year is about half the number of marriages that same year. But that's like computing the death rate by comparing the number of people who die with the number of people who are born.

That ignores those who neither were born nor died during that 12-month period. The 50 percent divorce figure ignores the number of intact marriages from years and decades earlier.

The truth is that about one of 50 marriages ends each year, according to the National Center for Health Statistics. Pollster Louis Harris maintains that 90 percent of marriages survive until one partner dies."

No doubt the spotlight has been in the wrong place and things are not as bad as they say.

First Things First

Relationships are easier to break than to make. That is why many give up so easily. We often set our relationships on automatic pilot – and wake up just before the crash.

Take the case of relational priorities with our spouses and children. Many get so focused on their children that they neglect their spouses – and end up with heartache. Janice Burns writes:

> *"The trait I most admired growing up was my mother's unwavering loyalty to my father. To the world, they presented a consolidated whole: respectful of each other, always each other's first priority.*
>
> *As a child, I wanted to be the center of my parents' universe. But my parents were, and are, each other's universe and we children remain merely sources of light that shine upon their special world.*
>
> *Only as an adult, can I appreciate the fact that although loved, we were not chosen in the way my parents chose each other."*

Burns' words are a wise reminder that, in our world of important relationships, we must always strive to keep first things first!

Four Words of Praise

I picked up my oldest son from school and asked, "How was your day?"

He answered enthusiastically, "It was great, Dad!"

"Why is that?" I asked.

"Today my teacher looked at my work and said I was doing an excellent job!" he explained. "Dad, that made my whole day."

And you know what? It made mine, too.

Funny, isn't it, how contagious a few, short words of praise can be. My son couldn't wait to pass on the satisfaction and pleasure he felt.

Experts tell us that we all need four words of praise for every one word of criticism to maintain a positive self-image. It is easy to notice when people do wrong – it takes a keen eye to notice when they do right.

Some work and home environments are faced with a praise shortage. Most of us try hard, and give our best, hoping that someone will notice.

If you see others mess up, bite your tongue – they usually figure it out, anyway!

On the other hand, if you see others do well, speak up! Chances are good that your words will make their day.

How Do You Spell Love?

Ask children this question, "How do you spell love?"
Do you know what is often the surprising answer?
T-I-M-E. There is no amount of talk, exciting events, or
gifts that can ever replace time well spent with children.

Talk to busy executives who work 90 hours a week and
ask, "Why do you do it?"

And their answer? "For my kids."

Look at their itineraries and see how often the word
"kids" appears.

I have met some of their kids. They tell me, "My dad
tries to buy me off. He's never around, so he brings me
gifts. I like getting stuff, but I see through it."

Bonding does not happen through the gifts we give, but
through the time we give. It has been well said that, "You
can fool a fool, you can con a con, but you can't kid a kid."

Children don't really want presents from their parents
as much as they want their parents' presence. The best
expression of love is time spent – quality and quantity.

Let's Hope We're
Man Enough

I've never seen anything quite like it. I was talking with Dave when his son came home from school.

Aaron, a strong, athletic 16-year-old walked over to his father, who was sitting in his easy chair, and sat in his lap. He then gave his dad a hug and asked, "How was your day, Dad?"

"Just fine, Son, how about you?" responded his dad.

"No problems. Well, I gotta run to baseball practice." And off he went.

I pulled my chin up off the floor and asked, "How did you manage *that?*"

"Manage what?" Dave asked.

"Well," I informed him, "it's not every day that I see a macho 16-year-old sit in his dad's lap and give him a hug in front of a stranger."

"Oh, that," Dave replied. "When Aaron was about ten-years-old, I had a little talk with him. I told him that right now he still thought I was fairly cool but that the days were coming when that opinion might start to slip. I shared that I would have to make some tough decisions, especially in his teen years, and he would probably get frustrated with me. I told him that I had felt that way with my dad, too. I told him that I believed that, if we're man enough, we could continue to show each other this love. Therefore, each day we try to give each other a hug and say, 'I love you.' I believe this will help us through the times when we don't see eye to eye."

"Well, Dave, it seems to be working," I observed.

"So far, so good," he replied.

On my way home, I thought of my sons. At the time, my oldest son was 10. I determined to have the same talk with him. When the time was right, I did. Now, he is 20-years-old. So far, so good.

Soft Answer

I was conversing with a group of teenagers about getting along with their parents, when one boy presented a tough scenario.

"What should I do about my mom?" he asked. "She is always yelling at me. Every day when I get home I get nonstop haranguing."

"Have you ever tried the 'soft reply?'" I asked. I paused and explained, "When someone's volume is up, the best way to bring it down is to answer softly – in complete control. Gently respond with something like, 'OK, Mom, I'll take care of that.'"

"I don't know," he answered. "I guess it's worth a try."

"Let me know what happens," I said.

Later he told me, "I came home and sure enough she jumped all over me, yelling about this and that. Usually I would yell back and get into trouble. But today I answered, 'OK Mom, I'll take care of it.'

'What did you say?' she asked.

'I'll take care of it,' I answered, completely in control.

"And, do you know what she did?" he asked.

"No," I answered. "What?"

"She went and found my brother and started yelling at him!" he answered, smiling from ear to ear.

He had found the old proverb to be true: "A soft answer turns away anger."

Promise Keepers

I sat down with my family to talk about the kind of values we wanted to have have in our home and the rules we could and should live by – sort of a family mission statement.

The children came up with a number of good suggestions, but there was one I was especially impressed with: "Always keep your promises."

I thought to myself, "Well, they've been hearing my sermons after all."

Then came the moment of truth. I asked my children, "Which of these suggestions do you think I need the most work on?"

My 10-year-old son offered, "The one about keeping promises."

I was stunned! Keeping my promises is something I have always worked hard to achieve. Trying not to be defensive, I asked, "When did I break a promise to you?"

He answered, "I remember once you said you were going to buy me goldfish crackers, and you didn't."

"Goldfish crackers! How old were you when that happened?" I asked.

"I was four, Dad," he quickly replied.

I was doubly stunned. It was not like I promised Disney World and reneged; but six years later, he still remembered the grocery treat I flippantly promised and somehow forgot. The important thing was that he remembered.

Children aren't impressed so much with the words we speak, as they are with the words we keep.

The Time to Laugh

When we hurt are probably the most difficult times to laugh; but oddly enough, those are the times that we need humor the most.

I remember being laid up in the hospital with tubes sticking out of my lung cavity. It was painful to breathe – and it was torture to laugh. I became depressed and frustrated with my condition.

My friend, Scott, came to see me in the visitors' lounge. I begged him, "Please, Scott, no jokes – it's too painful. If you can't refrain for my sake, do it for this woman here!" (I pointed to the lady next to me with broken ribs, who was in pretty bad shape).

So what did he do? He delivered 20 minutes of the best comedy material either of us had ever heard. We were wheezing, coughing, waving him off, and begging him to stop. We laughed ourselves practically into a coma. The laughter was killing our bodies, but refreshing our souls.

Scott and I have stayed in regular contact for over two decades, despite 2,000 miles of separation. I have learned that the best friend you can have in this world is the person who will make you laugh – when you least want to.

It's Great to Be Great

I still remember the thrill, as a young teenager, when my father took me to a major league baseball game. We went extra early and I stood right at the fence to get a close-up view of my heroes.

There was a young player on the opposing team that I recognized. "Mr. So and So," I politely asked, "could I please have your autograph?"

He never said a word – he didn't have to. He rolled his eyes, turned up his nose, and walked off with a "Humph."

I was stunned. During the game, I could not keep myself from hoping he would strike out, but he didn't. He went on to a long and distinguished career. I could never get myself to cheer for his team, however, because of the sudden fame that had obviously over-inflated his head.

In later years, I would meet many professional athletes and so-called famous folks. Some treated me with dignity and respect, while others were patronizing or even downright rude.

The whole experience reminds me of the words of Will Rogers, "It's great to be great, but it's greater to be human."

Doing a Little More

These days there seems to be a lot more talk about values, character, and virtue. There is a danger with so much lofty talk: people begin to allow ideals to replace actions.

Great thoughts are empty if not accompanied by great action. No matter how much good we are presently doing, we need to be challenged by the thought that we could and can do more. William Arthur Ward wrote:

"I will do more than belong
I will participate.
I will do more than care
I will help.
I will do more than believe
I will practice.
I will do more than be fair
I will be kind.
I will do more than forgive
I will forget.
I will do more than dream
I will work."

Indeed, it is great to possess kind thoughts and feel noble emotions, but it is even greater to act on those feelings!

Father's Day Cards

Some time ago, a prison ministry group decided to try an unusual project. To help the prisoners begin communicating with their families, they decided to provide them with Mother's Day and Father's Day cards.

The group approached a greeting card company who agreed to supply the cards at no cost.

Much to the surprise of everyone, the program was a great success. Prisoners responded enthusiastically. After one year, the group was asked by the card company if they were ready to reorder.

"Yes," the coordinator replied, "all the Mother's Day cards were sent and they need a whole new supply."

"And, how many Father's Day cards will they need?" the representative asked.

He paused for a moment and then said, "It's strange, but not one Father's Day card was sent!"

Out of hundreds of inmates given the opportunity, not one had a significant enough relationship with his father to send a card.

We can learn a powerful lesson from those doing "hard time" about the impact of fathers who are willing to spend time with their children.

Maintenance Programs

How important is maintenance? An anonymous quote reads, "Spend the extra dollars to maintain your equipment, spend the extra time to maintain relationships. Remember, you don't have to brush all your teeth, either – only the ones you want to keep."

It is so easy to focus on the "new and improved" and different that we forget the importance of maintaining what we have – and strengthening that which remains.

If something breaks, most people just throw it out and get a new one. We are a consumer society; people do not think much about fixing or repairing. Maintenance is not important in such a society. A cheap gadget is one thing; the relationship with your family and friends is an altogether different matter.

Most things do not stay in good condition on their own, but require attention and maintenance – whether it is changing the oil or salving a wound. Likewise, relationships stay in good condition because we care for and pay attention to them.

The best insurance to keep things from falling apart is a good maintenance program.

Random Acts of Kindness

Have you been victimized by the underground contagion spreading across our nation?

On a winter day in San Francisco, a woman drove up to a tollbooth and said, "I'm paying for myself and the six cars behind me." She then handed over seven commuter tickets.

This woman had read a saying that inspired her, "Practice random kindness and senseless acts of beauty."

It seemed to be a message from above. Others heard it and read it and began doing such things as:

- Painting classrooms in depressed schools
- Leaving hot meals in a poor part of town
- Slipping money into a proud, old widow's purse
- Picking up litter and planting flower

These acts of kindness and beauty spread wildly, making the world a more beautiful place. Ghandi said:

"It's the action not the fruit of the action that's important. It may not be in your power or your time that there'll be any fruit. But that doesn't mean you stop doing the right thing. You may never know what results will come from your action. But if you do nothing, there will be no result."

Timmy, You're a Man Now

Every night, Tim was accustomed to his father coming into his room to tuck him in, give him a kiss, and say, "I love you."

One night when he was eight-years-old, his dad came in, stuck out his hand and said, "Timmy, you're a man now, you can shake Daddy's hand!"

Tim shook his hand and said, "OK, Dad."

Now a man, Tim told me, "Dad didn't know it, but I cried myself to sleep that night and lots of nights after that. He didn't kiss me or hug me after that, and he didn't say I love you' as freely, either. The love was still there, but he had begun to close the door on expressing it."

Tim paused and then said, "Today, I know that my father and I truly love each other. At moments when we see each other, our love for each other is visible in our eyes. Somehow, though, we don't quite know how to say it. The door has never been fully opened since that night many years ago."

I will never forget Tim's words as his story ended: "Eight- years-old is too young to become a man," he said, "and no one should become so much of a man that he can't show affection."

Spilled Milk

Stephen Glenn tells the story about a famous research scientist who was asked why he was so much more creative than his peers.

The scientist said that it all started with an experience he had when he was two-years-old. In trying to remove a large bottle of milk from the refrigerator, he lost his grip, which resulted in a sea of milk on the floor.

When his mother saw the spill, instead of yelling at him, she said, "What a great and wonderful mess. I've never seen such a milk puddle. The damage is done, would you like to play in it before we clean it up?"

So he did!

When he was done playing, his mother said to him, "You know, whenever you make a mess, you have to clean it up. So how would you like to do it? A towel, a sponge, or a mop?"

He chose the sponge and together they cleaned up the mess.

After they were done cleaning, she said, "You know, we had a failed experiment in how to carry a big milk bottle."

So she took him and the bottle outside and let him practice with the bottle full of water. On his own, he discovered a way to carry it with his little hands.

This renowned scientist remarked that his success could be traced back to that incident – it was there that he learned not to be afraid of making mistakes.

What's in a Name?

Before our youngest child was born, my wife and I must have researched every "naming your baby" book ever published.

One of those books, *What's in a Name?*, lists about 700 first names and gives their literal meanings, character qualities, corresponding Scripture verses, and further explanations.

The introduction of the book tells an interesting story about a boy named Clayton, who was nicknamed Clay by his friends.

Clay's well-meaning, but misguided, uncle equated his name with "dirt." Because of this nickname, Clay had self-image and attitude problems – until the day he met Mr. John Hartzell, one of the book's compilers.

John explained that clay is not just dirt; it is an important substance, a raw material, that when placed in the potter's hands becomes a thing of beauty and usefulness.

Amazingly, this explanation helped Clayton take a different view of himself. He started to realize his own self-worth and uniqueness, and starting facing life with renewed vigor and attitude.

As sad as this story is, it holds meaning. Although his uncle meant no harm, he did harm. We can never underestimate the power of our words – even when spoken in jest.

Leaders Follow

S. T. McMillen tells a great story about a young woman who applied to a college.

The prospective student's heart sank when she read the question on the application blank, "Are you a leader?" Being both honest and conscientious, she wrote "no," returned the application, and expected the worst.

To her surprise, she received this letter from the college:

Dear Applicant:

A study of the application forms reveals that this year our college will have 1,452 new leaders. We are accepting you because we feel it is imperative that they have at least ONE follower.

A basic principle of leadership is that great leaders are developed by being great followers. We set great examples only when we follow great examples.

It is important to have a human model of character and conduct that we strive to follow – even if that model only lives in our memories.

Our world needs people willing to serve. Those who excel at serving somehow seem to end up at the front.

Radiate Friendship

Lowell Davis was a fellow who knew how to make friends. If you had ever met him, he would have known it because he would have written down your name.

He had a big, yellow legal pad on which he would write the name of every person he remembered meeting since he was three-years-old, along with a note about that person.

For example, he wrote, "Leonard McKnight likes chicken gravy."

In his notebook, Lowell had a list of names and notes numbering 3,487.

No matter what business you are in, to be successful, you must learn to excel in the people business.

Mr. Davis reveals something key about those who are successful in the people business. He was genuinely interested in people – and he radiated friendship!

He did not just want to know a person's name; he wanted to know something about that individual. He learned to look for the uniqueness in each person he met.

When we look for originality, everyone becomes interesting to meet and know. And that sort of interest is sure to come back; or, as Henry Davidson aptly stated, "Radiate friendship and it will be returned tenfold."

Keep It Simple

Two people selling almost identical products made back-to-back presentations. The first presenter impressed the group with his deep and profound knowledge of the complicated technology – lucidly bantering in multi-syllabic technocratic terms.

The second presenter spoke plainly and unimpressively about what the machines did and how they worked.

The second presenter got the sale.

One audience member challenged the second presenter saying that the first presenter was twice as smart.

Her reply, "No, he was twice as complex. I follow one rule, the *K.I.S.S. Rule* – 'Keep It Simple, Stupid.'"

There is nothing so profound as simplicity. People buy into what they understand.

Einstein was once asked to explain relativity. "Put your hand on a hot stove for a minute," he said, "and it seems like an hour, but sit with a pretty girl for an hour and it seems like a minute."

The truly smart person does not try to impress people with insider-industry jargon and obscure terms, but strives to make things understandable.

Or as Einstein put it, "Things should be made as simple as possible, but not any simpler."

Pleasing Nobody

There is an ancient fable about a man, a boy, and a donkey that illustrates a great lesson about people-pleasing.

The man and boy were walking to market with the donkey trailing behind. A farmer criticized them saying, "What good is the donkey if you don't ride it?"

So the boy rode on the donkey.

A man on the road criticized him saying, "Look at the lazy boy making his poor old father walk!"

So the boy got off and the father began to ride.

Two women noticed and said, "Did you ever see such a lazy man? He rides and takes ease while his son walks."

So they both rode together.

They came to town and the crowd jeered them, "You are cruel to that donkey. It's too much to carry you both."

The man was ashamed, so he came up with a plan. They tied the donkey's feet to a long pole and carried the donkey.

The donkey didn't like it much, but he couldn't help himself. People laughed at the funny sight.

When they came to a bridge, the donkey kicked a foot loose and the boy dropped his end of the pole, causing the donkey to fall off the bridge and into the river where he drowned.

"I think, my son," said the man, "that we may learn a lesson from all this."

"What kind of lesson, Father?" the boy asked.

The man answered, "Try to please everybody, and you will please nobody."

How You Treat Yourself

Have you ever met people who were mad at the world? Sure you have. They are the ones with the proverbial chip on their shoulders, a tight grimace upon their lips, and a scornful look upon their faces.

I met a young man like this. He seemed like a stick of dynamite just waiting for someone to light his fuse.

Risking his wrath, I asked, "What's the problem?"

"No respect," he complained. "I just want a little respect!"

I thought to myself what I am sure everyone else was thinking, "What's to respect here?" He doesn't smile, and he isn't friendly. He looks angry, his words are sharp, and he stays to himself. He offers nothing positive, shows no self-respect, but *he wants respect!*

Respect is, more or less, a mirror. People reflect what we give to them.

Martin Rutle said, "You train people how to treat you by how you treat yourself."

Rowing Together

The Americans and the Japanese decided to engage in a competitive boat race. Both teams practiced hard and long. The Japanese won by a mile. The American team was discouraged by the loss, and their morale sagged. Management decided that they had to find a reason for the crushing defeat, so they hired a consulting firm to investigate the problem. The consultants' findings:

- The Japanese team had eight people rowing and one person steering.
- The American team had one person rowing and eight people steering.

After a year of study and millions spent, the consulting firm concluded, "Too many people were steering on the American team."

As race day neared the following year, the American team's structure was completely reorganized. The new structure was one steersman, one steering manager, four assistant steering managers, one overall crew manager, and a performance review manager to analyze the efficiency of the person rowing the boat.

This time, the Japanese won by *two* miles!

Humiliated, the Americans fired the rower for poor performance and gave the managers a bonus for discovering the problem.

Whenever there is a problem, it can usually be solved by people rowing together.

BUILDING RELATIONSHIPS

Strength in Weakness

It was perhaps the most unusual resume he had ever received. The executive told me that, at first, it looked like any resume – experience, skills, and references – until the end, where the applicant listed, "Liabilities: impatience, sometimes overly candid, easily frustrated with detail work, etc."

This executive said, "I've never seen before a resume that listed an applicant's weaknesses. We were impressed enough to hire him."

"Why?" I asked.

His answer was telling.

"Any individual who is not afraid to list his liabilities on his resume tells us a number of things about him," the executive said. "First, the individual is very confident. Second, the individual is not pretentious. Third, the individual is realistic about what he can and cannot do. And, fourth, the individual is honest about his own capabilities."

It is amazing how much strength they read into that list of weaknesses!

People who are truly comfortable with who they are have learned that it is far easier to admit their weaknesses than it is to conceal or make excuses for their shortcomings. For it is in admitting our weaknesses that we show our true strength.

Simple Expectations

I stayed at a resort that is frequented by a variety of corporate groups from all over the nation.

I began talking to the hotel desk clerks because I was curious about their observations of the diverse people they serve each day. I asked them, "What is the *best* group of people you've ever served?"

One clerk quickly answered, "It's not even close – it's a company that comes here each year, whose business is primarily to the rural areas."

"What sets them apart from other groups?" I asked.

"In a word, it is gratitude," he answered. "Most of the groups that come have individuals that go ballistic if every detail is not perfect. But, not in this group. Everyone is thankful for every good thing. Maybe it's because of their simple, non-cluttered lifestyle. They are thrilled with every little service or amenity we offer."

His answer illustrated how easily most of us have become spoiled and intolerant of the inevitable human fallibility.

Happiness is often just a case of making simple things matter.

Mutual Respect

In the book, *Training a Tiger,* Earl Woods, father of golf phenomenon, Tiger Woods, talks about how he built a solid relationship with his son.

He wrote, "The relationship between parent and child must be built on mutual respect. Convey to the child that you care, that you are there like an oak in support. Above all, be consistent. A child can be thrown off by waffling."

He also addresses priorities: "It's not always easy in this age of 2-job households to spend time with your child. I believe time is a product of one's priorities. If your priority is your child, you will find time."

Earl's policy was if the kid wanted to talk, the TV, the stereo, whatever, went off. They went to another room and he *listened* to his child.

When Tiger Woods won his first Masters, without hesitation and with millions watching, he instinctively ran into the arms of his parents and held them – and we all saw the rewards of mutual respect.

Test of Love

Sue Walter Scott wrote, "In lovers' quarrels, the party that loves most is always most willing to acknowledge the greater fault."

It is a sort of "test of love" – the "winner" is the one who is quicker and more willing to admit culpability, and to repair the relationship and move on.

Few topics have inspired as many cynical words as love and marriage.

One person wrote, "When a marriage ends in divorce, it is merely another fight that hasn't gone the distance."

Shakespeare wrote, "When I said, 'I would die a bachelor,' I did not think I should live till I was married."

Still another wrote, "Marriage, which makes the two one, is a lifelong struggle to discover which is that one!"

No two individuals could possibly bring their love, lives, dreams, pasts, and hurts into one arena and not see that love tested. So, Sir Walter Scott's words give all lovers an acid test for our love: Are we willing to admit faults? Are we willing to move on?

Love that has been tested is the strongest love of all.

Emphatically Yours

How hard can you be on others and still treat yourself right? If you cannot forgive others, will you be able to move on past your own mistakes?

The ability to express compassion and to live with empathy toward others is a serious cornerstone for success.

If you do not possess the patience or desire to listen to others, soon they will have no desire to listen to you. If you have trouble understanding or validating the feelings of others, soon they will act robotic and emotionless towards you.

Successful people are those who understand that all people treat one view as most important – their own!

Empathy is the ability to see and feel events from the other person's perspective. Once we've been there, it is easy.

A simple rule for success and progress is: You will get a whole lot further in this world by attempting to walk in other peoples' shoes.

Communicate

In an interview with a very successful businesswoman, I asked, "Why do some business relationships have great success while others turn out to be miserable failures?"

"One word," she replied. "Communication. Successful relationships are built on the idea that we assume nothing. Failed relationships begin with communication, but regress to the point where the 'left hand knows not what the right hand is doing.'"

We all can point to numerous examples of the fallout due to a lack of communication in our own relationships.

We have learned many lessons on communication through the "School of Hard Knocks:"

- We didn't listen well enough.
- We assumed that we understood what someone wanted.
- We thought we told someone what we were doing.
- As much as we talk, we still need to communicate more.

Successful communicators follow some simple but profound rules: assume nothing, return communiques promptly, and ask – even if you think you already know.

Lead, Don't Drive

There are two countries in the Mid-East that border one another. Both countries have large sheep and mutton industries. Even though the terrain and landscape are essentially the same, one country's sheep industry prospers while the other country's industry struggles.

Industry experts wondered how this could be. When they studied the two industries, they found only one major difference: In one country, the shepherd walks in front of the sheep, and in the other, the shepherd walks behind the sheep.

The nation that prospers is the country where the shepherds walk in front. They lead their sheep, not drive them. Sheep can wander occasionally for better grass or water and catch up later with the flock. These sheep have initiative and, as a result, are healthier and fatter.

In the country where they drive the herd, the sheep are hit over the head at just one step out of pattern. Some sheep become so lethargic that they can stand in grass two feet high and not eat.

The obvious lesson here is that leaders get much better results than drivers – or coercive-type managers. Or, as one fellow put it, "If you want to know if you are truly a leader, look behind you. If there is no one following, you are not a leader – no matter what your resume or title says."

The Debate Rule

Imagine a child saying to a parent, "Don't question what I say – I'm the child around here and you'll do what I tell you."

Sounds ludicrous, doesn't it? But, it does not seem any less ludicrous to children who hear their parents say these words. If being older automatically makes us right, then there would no such thing as an "old fool."

In our home, we have instituted a rule with the children called the "debate rule." It works this way: When the adult is giving an order or sounding a final opinion and the children do not understand or agree, they can politely announce, "I'd like to debate."

The key here is courtesy.

The first debate arose with one of my sons over, of all things, whose turn it was to clean the cat's litter box. I had already issued an order, and my son calmly debated his point.

And, guess what? He was right. It made me wonder how many other times he had been right, but had no opportunity to speak.

A rule of thumb for relationships is that people are more willing to listen to us when they know we are willing to listen to them.

Significant Others

I once read about a nursing student who got a real surprise on a pop quiz. She had no problems with any of the questions until she came to the last one: "What is the first name of the woman who cleans the school?"

She thought it was a joke. She had seen the cleaning woman a number of times, but she couldn't possibly be expected to know her name. She handed in her paper and left the last question blank.

Before the class was over, one of the students asked if that particular question would count toward their grades.

"Absolutely," replied the professor. "In your careers you will meet many people. Each individual is significant, and deserves your attention and care – even if all you do is smile and say, 'Hello.'"

This professor, in an unusual manner, was trying to teach her students that success requires not only technical knowledge, but a sincere interest in people as well.

This particular student never forgot that valuable lesson.

Oh, and by the way, she also learned that the cleaning woman's name was Dorothy!

Focus on Strengths

I once asked a business manager what he was doing to help improve his employees' performance.

He answered, "I'm pointing out their weaknesses and showing them where they need to improve."

"Good luck," I grunted.

"What do you mean?" he shot back.

"All you are doing," I offered, "is acting as a mirror for what these people already know and do not like. You have become a reminder of everything they find distasteful about themselves."

Leadership author Joe Batten put it this way, "A fault or weakness is a void, a nothing, a shortage of or an absence of a strength."

To help people improve, we must focus on their strengths. Show them how to develop certain strengths, and encourage them by reminding them of the strengths they already have.

We all like hearing about our strengths and talents, rather than having our faces rubbed in the mire of our all-too-evident shortcomings.

Try changing your focus today. Start looking for strengths in your spouse, children, and friends. Focus on their strengths, and see what you have been missing!

My Brother's Brother

Joe Batten, truly one of the world's great thinkers on the issue of leadership, is the man who gave the phrase, "Be all you can be," to the U.S. Army.

But Batten gave another phrase that had an even greater impact.

In 1969, Batten was invited by chief leaders in South Africa to conduct leadership training. He was immediately stricken with the harsh realities of Apartheid and the fact that white leaders sincerely thought they were doing the right thing. In fact, they told him that South Africa was the most Christian Nation on Earth. They were proud that they gave the "non-whites" food, shelter, and good air.

Batten asked the group of leaders, "How many of you believe you are your brother's keeper?"

They all raised their hands.

Batten responded, "I don't believe in being my brother's keeper. I want to be my brother's brother and teach him to keep himself."

Before Batten left South Africa, the saying had spread like wildfire throughout the nation – and for over two decades it grew. This ethos became the philosophical underpinning for the eventual disassembling of Apartheid.

The More the Merrier

What's the best cure for the common cold virus? A cup of chicken soup? According to a study in the *Journal of the American Medical Association,* it may be the friend who brings the soup.

A recent study, led by Professor Sheldon Cohen, found that the more diverse your sets of relationships are, the less likely you are to catch a cold. People with six or more types of relationships had 1/4 the risk of becoming sick as those people with only one to three types of relationships.

This study is part of a growing field known as psychoneuro-immunology – the study of how factors such as stress and social support affect the immune system and overall health.

Cohen's study found that susceptibility to a virus is related to such stresses as job hassles or a death in the family.

According to Dr. Herbert Benson, it seems quite possible that diverse social ties decrease stress. Stress liberates hormones in our body, which in turn lowers our resistance to illness.

Diversity seems to be the key here. It is not just the number of people, but the number of different social roles.

A rule of thumb for staying healthy seems to be "the more the merrier!"

Careful About Assumptions

The assumptions we have about other people can come back to haunt us.

For example, if we catch what we think is a negative look from someone, our minds start to race and come up with all manner of reasons for the look. We might think to ourselves, "He doesn't like me!" or "She heard something about me!" or "He thinks he's better than I!"

Once filled with such assumptions, we begin to plan a response based on what we already have talked ourselves into believing. We may act cold, indifferent, offended, or disinterested the next time we see the individual – and guess what? That person begins to wonder what got into *us!*

If we were to talk to this individual, we would most likely discover that the original negative look that upset us had nothing to do with us. The individual may have been thinking intensely – which was reflected in his facial expression.

These scenarios happen every day. Our own insecurities and fears can cause us to read the worst in a random look or word.

It is best to turn off assumptions before the snowball starts down-hill. I have found that one of the worst forms of exercise is "jumping to conclusions."

Sincerely

Pottery makers in the days of old had a system for guaranteeing integrity to their customers. If a pot was flawless, they would stamp a word on the bottom that translates "sincere" or "no hidden flaws."

"Insincere" potters would pour wax into a crack and paint over it. When the unwary buyer poured a hot liquid into the pot, it would melt the wax and reveal a crack in the pot (which, by the way, is where we got the term, "crackpot").

This background look at the root of the word, "sincere," gives a vivid word-picture and lesson concerning personal sincerity and integrity.

Insincerity has a way of revealing itself when the heat is on. If there is a flaw in ourselves or in our work, we are best to reveal ourselves.

Sincerity is the basis for trust and trust is the basis for success. Being up-front means that if there is a crack in the pot, we are the one to expose it.

Ann Morrow Lindbergh said, "There is nothing more exhausting than insincerity."

"I Was Wrong"

The other day I was at a business meeting when I asked an associate about a matter that I thought I had asked her to resolve.

She quickly responded, "No, you didn't!" and began telling me the facts as she saw them.

Others were watching our conversation and waiting for, what they thought would be, the inevitable argument over who was supposed to do what.

I thought about her version of the story and realized that she was right. I said, "I'm sorry, I was wrong."

One observer in the office asked, "What did you just say?"

"I was wrong," I answered.

"Excuse my shock," she said, "but I don't hear too many people admit they are wrong."

"Well," I assured her, "I've had plenty of opportunity to practice – having been wrong so many times."

Why are the words, "I was wrong" so hard to say? Are we afraid this will be news to anyone? The easier we admit our errors, the quicker we will be able to fix the problem.

The most efficient way to make things right is to be at ease admitting, "I was wrong."

Rattlesnakes and Earthquakes

Dale Carnegie said, "There is only one way to get the best of an argument - and that is to avoid it. Avoid it as you would avoid rattlesnakes and earthquakes. Nine times out of ten an argument ends with each of the contestants being more firmly convinced than ever that he is absolutely right."

Like rattlesnakes, arguments usually result in an exchange of venom. Enduring bitterness over poisonous tones or words overshadow whatever relationship existed before the incident.

Like earthquakes, arguments and contentions can swallow us, and we become immersed and obsessed with the debate. And for what purpose? To prove ourselves right and the other person wrong? Or to gloat in the victory? By doing so, we create a great chasm that will be difficult to cross.

It has been said, "Argue with a man against his will, and he will walk away of the same opinion still."

As Dale Carnegie reminded us, the only way to win in arguments is, as with rattlesnakes and earthquakes, to keep a safe distance from them.

Playful Spirits

Relax, You May Only Have a Few Minutes Left! is the title of a book by Loretta LaRoche. She contends that most of us have not yet discovered how to use the power of humor to overcome stress in our lives and jobs.

LaRoche suggests that we adopt a more playful approach to life. Have fun with life. Do some silly things. Get some of the starch out. Use your imagination.

For example, LaRoche carries a Groucho Marx nose mustache and glasses in her car. When she is driving through busy traffic and needs to change lanes, she puts the glasses on – and sure enough, the other drivers let her in! Of course, you do not have to do outrageous things, just keep your mind open to fun and creative thoughts and impulses.

Another expression of playfulness is to do something nice when someone least expects it. For example, give unexpected flowers or cards, or pay for the person behind you at the drive-thru. The smile on the other person's face makes it all worthwhile.

Playful spirits keep that imaginative childlike wonder toward life. Learn to relax – because you truly do not know how much time you have.

No Ordinary People

Harold and Evelyn Lincoln were undoubtedly two of the most fascinating and extraordinary people I've had the pleasure of knowing.

Evelyn was the personal secretary to John F. Kennedy for 12 years and was privy to every major meeting and decision in his career. Her husband, Harold, an influential lawyer in the Bobby Kennedy Administration, was attorney general.

This couple knew everyone and everything in Washington, D.C. In short, these were two very important people. But what struck me most about them was how they treated each person they met as the most important person in the world.

They talked about how fascinated they were with people – they found all people truly interesting.

A result of their attitude toward people was their boundless energy, vision, and excitement for life – both of them living highly active lives well into their 80's.

They were never bored. They never lacked purpose. And they were students of the human race. They passed on a rare legacy – one which I hope I never forget – that we only become ordinary people by believing that there is such a thing as an ordinary person.

Listen with Your Face

BUILDING RELATIONSHIPS

I recently overheard one father telling a story about coming home after a hard day's work and plopping down into his easy chair to relax with the newspaper.

One of his sons entered and started to tell him what he thought was a fairly important event in his day.

Dad "listened" to the story while continuing to scan the newspaper.

Frustrated, the son burst out, "Dad, please put the paper down. I'm trying to tell you something."

"I'm listening, Son," he said. "I could repeat everything back to you."

"But, Dad," he pleaded, "I want you to listen with your face."

Kids do say the darnedest and wisest things, don't they?

I think of my own mannerisms and, like other multi-taskers, I always need to be doing two things at once – talking on the phone and writing; or organizing and straightening up while talking to a family member.

Some people feel that if they are not doing two things at one time, then they are not being productive – which can drive other people crazy!

Listen with your face. People want to see your eyes, which show you are sincerely interested; and your facial response, which demonstrates participation – to know for sure that their words have been heard.

Just Think

In his book, *The Road Less Traveled and Beyond,*
M. Scott Peck contends that most of us do not spend
enough time thinking. He states:

> *"The biggest difference between us humans and the
> other mammals is the size of our brains, and specifically
> of the part known as frontal lobes. These lobes are
> involved in our ability to make judgments, and it is here
> that thinking takes place. The point is that we don't use
> them enough. Because of laziness, fear or pride, we don't
> put our brains to full use. We are faced with the task of
> being fully human by taking more time to just think."*

Many people would say, "I wish I had time to just sit
around and think, but I'm just too busy."

The truth is, thinking is hard work. Thinking requires
us to look down the road, search every angle, and ponder
the possibility that we could be wrong.

Many people like to avoid this kind of "work." With
more thinking, however, we probably would do less
running around, experience less conflict, and feel a greater
sense of purpose.

Time to think is time well spent – just think of the
possibilities.

Fishing and Hunting

In recent years, experts from the Department of Natural Resources have lamented the decline of the percentages of people who engage in hunting and fishing activities with their children. There has been a steady drop in the last 20 years.

The number one reason parents give for not taking their children on these excursions is that they do not have enough time. Ironically, this is the same excuse teenagers give for not going fishing or hunting with their parents.

It was actually my oldest son who interested me in the outdoors. From the time he could talk, he spoke about fish, ducks, and wildlife – and that is not all bad. One local deputy told me he had never arrested a kid who had a fishing license in his pocket.

As a dad, I feel fortunate that I was there to see the excitement on my son's face when he shot his first duck, caught that five-pound large mouth bass, and caught his limit for the first time.

When a 16-year-old boy says to his father – as mine did to me – "Dad, I think you and I should go together for the duck opener this year; and every year let's make it a tradition," you know there is something magical about fishing and hunting.

The Empty Box

Can two unfulfilled people come together and suddenly fulfill one another? Apparently not, is the conclusion if we are to learn anything from high divorce rates and failed relationships. Dr. J. Allan Peterson writes:

> *"Marriage is an empty box. There is nothing in it. Marriage was never intended to do anything for anybody. People are expected to do something for marriage. If you do not put more into the box than you take out, it becomes empty. Love, romance, consideration, generosities aren't in marriage, they are in people and people put them into marriage."*

The failure rate of relationships speaks as much of false expectations as anything else. Many enter marriage believing it will be a 1+ 1 = 2 proposition, and end up with a 1 - 1 = 0 reality because they expect the other person to fill their emptiness.

When two full people look to fulfill one another, only then do they end up with a 1 + 1 = 11 reality – where the sum is truly greater than its parts.

You receive no more than you bring into a relationship.

"How Are You?"

"How are you?" You may hear that question a dozen times today. I want you to try something different. I want you to listen to your response to that almost automatic greeting. Ask yourself, "What does my answer sound like? Does it represent who I am?"

Some of the most common answers are, "I'm fine," or "I'm O.K.," or "Not bad." Does that mean we are good, simply because we are not bad? Maybe we should just answer, "Not dead!"

Author Joe Batten says we need to use grander words if we want to be grand people. Great people use great words. Responses such as, "I'm having a great time," or "Excellent," or "Wonderful," are more stimulating.

I was recently walking around town with my father when someone asked him, "How are you?"

"Sunny, like the weather," he answered as he smiled.

She smiled back and said, "That's a nice answer."

His bright answer to "How are you?" brightened her day.

"How would you have answered if the weather was lousy?" I asked.

"Sunny *un*like the weather," he responded with a grin.

Sosa's Sign

When Sammy Sosa, the Chicago Cubs slugger, comes to bat, he gives two separate signs. One is for his mother and the other is for deceased hall-of-fame broadcaster, Harry Carey.

When asked why he gives a sign for Harry Carey before every at-bat, Sosa gets a bit emotional. "When I was a young ballplayer and came to Chicago," Sosa says, "I thought I could be a good player. Harry came to me and said, 'Sammy, you have the stuff to be one of the great ones.' Harry could never know what those words meant to me."

Dr. George W. Crane once wrote, "Appreciative words are the most powerful force for goodwill on earth."

Nagging about another person's failures seems to do little more than cause disintegration and breakdown; but the celebration of positive virtues and a person's potential is like a signpost pointing forward.

Tennyson wrote, "We all need somebody to help us see what we can become."

For Sammy Sosa, those persons were his mother and Harry Carey.

Every time Sosa comes to bat and gives his signal to his mother in the Caribbean, and to Harry Carey in Heaven, he reminds us of the importance of encouragement.

Fighting Out

The farmer observed the young boy's fascination with the cocoon. After a long hibernation, the caterpillar was about to emerge a new creature. The boy could hardly contain his excitement as he watched the butterfly attempt to break its bonds.

The boy soon began to worry because he thought it wasn't happening fast enough, and the process looked too difficult. He was afraid that the butterfly wasn't strong enough to break out of the cocoon, so he decided to help by tearing open the cocoon.

The farmer warned the boy, but he insisted. He could not bear to watch the struggle any longer.

A sad and dejected boy came to the farmer later that day holding a deceased butterfly in his hands.

"Why did he die?" he asked through his tears.

"He died," the farmer explained, "because you helped him when you shouldn't have. The butterfly gets its strength for life in its fight out of the cocoon."

We are all tempted, at times, to overprotect; to buffer those we love in difficult struggles. We are like that child. The farmer's wisdom is in realizing that our struggles give us the power to survive.

Give the Chickens Their Space

The lady seated next to me on the airplane told me that anyone who grew up on a farm could tell what was wrong with today's society.

She said that all the fighting, bickering, and violence were due to the fact that folks just did not have enough space.

"Spend some time watching chickens," she offered. "They're fine until you start confining their space and fencing them in. Then they start pecking at each other and squawking. Soon it is all-out war."

"Now," my barnyard philosopher continued, "look at our cities and suburbs. We build houses on top of each other. We sit in traffic jams and spend an average of five years of our life waiting in lines. Anyone who grew up in the country can tell you that, to keep your sanity, you've got to have some space."

Those of us who live amongst the masses need to make a point of getting a little of this "space therapy." It helps us to think and to keep our priorities straight.

Or, as an old farmer once told me, "People are a lot like manure. When you pile them up, you get a stink. But, when you spread them out, they can do some good!"

Perfect Strangers

Spending a day with Ed was an education. Ed's schedule was tight and demanding – tasks to complete, places to go, and people to meet.

At noon, he was scheduled to meet with a group of prospective clients. They were all perfect strangers, but he quickly won them over with his graciousness, charm, and ready wit.

By 6:00 p.m., the day had taken his toll. Mentally and physically exhausted, he came home to find his wife and children waiting at the dinner table. The kids were a bit obnoxious, and Ed yelled something at them about keeping their voices down. He then muttered something to his wife about passing the potatoes.

What is wrong with this picture? We all know because we've been there. The question we ask ourselves is, "Why is it easier, at times, to treat perfect strangers with more kindness and courtesy than cherished family members?"

It is awfully easy to forget who all our hard work is for. The perfect rule, for our family members, might be to afford them the same courtesies we would offer a perfect stranger!

False Humility

There is perhaps no human trait rarer, or more needed, than humility. People genuinely struggle with this idea. In fact, most people opt for the counterfeit, "false humility," which is actually chocolate-covered arrogance.

To be truly humble, we must first understand what arrogance is:

1. Arrogance assumes that because we cannot imagine how something can be done, it must be impossible.
2. Arrogance does all of the talking and none of the listening.
3. Arrogance rejects advice because someone else said it, or because our minds are made up, or because we do not want someone else to get the credit.
4. Arrogance is the refusal to accept help, and the inability to accept a compliment. This is actually false humility at its best – or worse.

In these terms, we see that we all have some level of arrogance to overcome. On the other hand, humility instructs us that:

1. We need the input and help of others because we cannot possibly know or do everything.
2. We should give credit and accept compliments. It is arrogance that makes us weak and humility that makes us strong.

Don't Argue with a Fool

When I was younger, I loved a good argument. If I wasn't sure that I was right at the start of the argument, I was absolutely certain by the end of it.

My brother and I would watch the political talk shows and begin our own heated arguments. We thought this was what smart people did.

Arguing may be the biggest waster of our time, efforts, thoughts, and energies. It has been said, "Argue against a man against his will and he will be of the same opinion still."

Think about it. You will not find yourself in an argument with a wise person because that person is too wise to enter strife.

You will not make any progress arguing with a fool because a fool refuses to change his mind, anyway.

If you argue with an enemy, you will come away with a greater enemy. If you argue with a friend, you may come away with one less friend.

Argument produces very little fruit; and the fruit it does produce is rotten.

Winning an argument is an oxymoron; even if you win, your loss outweighs your gain.

Why Whales Jump

"Have you ever wondered how the whale trainers at Sea World get a 19,000 pound whale to jump 22 feet out of the water?"

This is a question that speaker Charles Coonradt likes to ask parents, coaches, and business managers.

Coonradt says that the typical American manager would start the whale training process by putting the rope immediately up to 22 feet. (There is no sense in celebrating shortcomings, right?) They call this goal setting.

The whale would be placed above the rope at 22 feet – and it would just sit there.

How do they do it at Sea World? They start by placing the rope *below* the surface so that the whale cannot fail. The whale gets immediate reinforcement – fish and pats on the back.

What if the whale goes under the rope? There are no electrocutions or other warnings in its personal file. Positive reinforcement is the cornerstone that produces spectacular results. The rope is raised slowly enough so that the whale does not starve – either physically or emotionally.

The lesson we can learn, according to Coonradt, is to *over-celebrate* and *under-criticize*. Make a big deal out of the good (and little) stuff, and be consistent.

People know when they screw up. What they need is help.

As author Tom Peters said, "Celebrate what you want to see more of."

You See What You Look For

Have you ever found yourself in a circumstance that was comically profound? Years ago, I was riding around with a friend who had been in law enforcement just long enough to believe every person on the street had some sort of criminal intent.

At first I thought he was joking with his comments, but I soon realized he was completely serious.

"Look at that guy over there," he pointed out. "He looks like a perp. And that one, I ought to follow him."

Almost everyone was suspect.

As we entered a shopping center, he became disturbed with the driver in front of him. He exclaimed, "Look at those license plates!" He leaned over to look, "They look fishy, and he's not driving properly."

So busy was he gathering evidence on the driver in front of him, that he did not notice where he was headed. Up on a curb we went – and my police officer friend just missed hitting a light pole!

I laughed until it hurt, but my serious friend did not see any humor in the situation. This scenario opened up a profound truth for me:

- It is unhealthy to be suspicious of everyone.
- We need to trust others until they prove unworthy.

Suspicion usually reveals more about the observer than it does the suspect. Ultimately in life, people see only what they are looking for.

Make the Most of the Moment

Maybe you have witnessed a scene like this: You are sitting in a restaurant on a Friday night and, like many other couples in the restaurant, you want to wind down from your long work week and catch up with one another.

You notice a man and woman at an adjacent table. The man is throwing some curt instructions at the server, and it appears that he has been waiting too long for his drink. Next, he is annoyed because he had requested his salad dressing on the side – and had waited too long for that.

His wife looks like she wants to crawl under the table. Whatever illusions of grandeur she had harbored for this evening had come crashing to the floor.

When you experience this sequence of events, you might feel justified in chiding the help. But when you watch someone else carry it out, you realize that:

1. You are not here for the salad as much as for each other.
2. Life is too short to ruin pleasant occasions by being short and demanding.
3. Little aggravations should never be allowed to spoil meaningful moments.

Leave It to the Birds

One summer it was almost impossible to sleep past 6:00 a.m. at our house. Every day at that time, a female cardinal would start nose-diving into our bedroom window.

The bird was unrelenting. Time after time she crashed beak-first into a reflection of her own image in the window. The female cardinal thought that some other bird had come to threaten her nest.

This reminds me of human nature. There are so many personality traits about others that irritate us. The annoyances that bother us the most and arouse attack, however, seem to be those characteristics that remind us of our own shortcomings. The greatest irritants are often the very things we despise in ourselves.

It is not easy to accept that what we perceive to be the enemy could be nothing more than a clear reflection of ourselves at our worst.

It is best to tend to our own nests. Attacking others, who seem to be a threat, is best left to the birds.

Remember Your "A-B-Cs"

I was out golfing with a friend and I could not help but admire his composure despite his apparent difficulties.

His shots were not going all that far, or even straight for that matter, yet he stayed as calm as a gentle breeze and got a little better on each shot.

Meanwhile, if I did not hit a shot just the way I wanted, I would respond like a cyclone and double my efforts on the next attempt, which further frustrated my efforts.

My friend was not playing his best, yet he was having fun. On the other hand, I was doing better, yet I was not having as pleasant a time as he was.

So I asked him, "How do you stay so cool after bad shots?"

He responded with a smile, "I just remember my 'A-B-Cs.'"

"And what are those?" I asked.

He explained, "Attitude, behavior, and control. I always focus my attitude on getting a good result on the next shot, not on despising the last one. I try to behave in a way that shows class and composure. And, finally, I try to control my emotions and my mouth."

As complicated as life can get, success is simple: "Attitude - Behavior - Control." All you need to know in life is your "A-B-Cs."

Joy in Annoyances

BUILDING RELATIONSHIPS

It is amazing how the things that annoy one person can bring joy to another. What brings aggravation to one brings fascination to another. Happiness, or haplessness, often hinges simply on our perspective of an event. Rich Fullerton wrote the following on this theme:

> *"While I was working inside the house, a garbage truck lumbered down our street. Stopping every few seconds to grind and crush the trash, the truck was incredibly noisy. It broke my concentration. Irked, I walked to the window hoping to speed the truck's passing with an annoyed glare.*
>
> *But in the front yard, my 5-year-old son was thrilled. I watched him climb on top of a fire hydrant near the street. From there he had the best possible view inside the back of the huge truck where giant mechanical teeth chewed up the garbage. The noise just made it more fascinating to him."*

It is a marvelous thing that five-year-olds can enjoy life by just watching garbage trucks, and that adults can enjoy life by just watching five-year-olds.

Know What Matters

People are often intimidated by those who have a lot of factual knowledge, especially those individuals who grandstand their superior intellect.

Many people learn just enough to make them dangerous. In our society, we place far too much emphasis on learning facts that do us little good.

The great inventor, Thomas Edison, was once asked how many feet were in a mile.

Edison replied, "I don't know. Why should I fill my mind with facts I can find in two minutes in any standard reference book?"

There is a powerful lesson here. It is more important to use our minds for thinking, than just as a warehouse for storing needless information.

There is little proof that any champion on *Jeopardy* was ever wildly successful in life. So, if you are one of those individuals who gets clobbered playing *Trivial Pursuit,* remember it is trivial!

Our minds serve us best not by storing, but by thinking about the things we really need to know to succeed in life.

The truly intelligent person knows those things.

Time and Money

It has been said that "time is money." But time is not money – time is time. Time only equals money to those who measure their lives in monetary terms.

Time, however, is a commodity and, as a commodity, it is ruled by the Law of Supply and Demand. When time is in the abundant supply of youth, it is often wasted away and even ignored.

When time is in short supply in the season of maturity, it is held dear and treasured. Time is ruled by supply and demand; the less you have, the more you will give for it.

Time is also ruled by inflation. The price always rises as time goes by.

The sands of time fall so quietly that hardly a soul notices until only a few grains remain. And, what do people ponder when the last, precious grains are falling? "How did I spend my money?" No, they contemplate, "How did I spend my time?"

There is no lottery available to gain an unlimited supply of time – the rich and the poor are given the same allotment.

View your time each day as your most precious commodity. Time is the wealth you will leave someday with those you love.

Showing Up

Woody Allen once said, "Eighty percent of success is just showing up." The more I see of both success and failure, the more I am inclined to agree.

One factor that continues to astound me is the little effort many people put forward for their own success. They become impatient and frustrated when asked to do little things like redoing, reworking, or rewriting. You will often hear, "If that's not good enough, then just forget it!"

What bestseller was published in first-draft form? What outstanding achievements in our lives are accomplished on the first go 'round? Look beneath the art of the masters and you will find many layers of paint.

"Showing up" means: keeping appointments; returning calls and correspondence; and studying the methods and secrets of those who have succeeded.

We can all think of missed opportunities where we dropped the ball or lacked proper follow-through. Success is not always a matter of great talent or great ideas, it is often a matter of just showing up.

FULFILLING

YOUR
POTENTIAL

Practice, Practice, Practice

As a teenager, I remember playing endless hours of basketball – four to eight hours a day, depending on the season. I had many heroes and I followed their advice to the letter.

"Pistol" Pete Maravich said to shoot 1,000 shots a day, so I did.

I especially remember the words of advice given by "Dollar" Bill Bradley, then of New York Knickerbockers fame, and now a New Jersey Senator.

He told of how, during his days at Princeton, his father would tell him, "Son, when you're not out practicing, someone else is. And when you meet that person, he's going to beat you."

Bradley determined that he would not be out-practiced. Other great athletes followed this same pattern. It was said of Larry Bird that he was always the first to the gym and the last one out.

Practice. It causes the difficult to become graceful, natural, and instinctive.

Talent and cleverness never replace practice. Good performances are always the result of good practice.

Expressing Who You Are

Have you ever had an experience where you put forth effort in a task, saw it completed, and felt an overwhelming sense of purpose and satisfaction in the execution of that task? If you have, you no doubt remember the experience.

Contrast that experience with those tasks you have been forced to complete that were absolute drudgery, stressful, and done with loathing. What was the difference?

In the first example, chances are that what you were doing was an expression of who you naturally are – the sum of your natural abilities, interests, and purpose in life. You were experiencing a total "life click," where all cylinders of your being were working harmoniously to achieve a task. This is the highest order of living and being.

In the negative example of drudgery and stress, you were more likely living out an expression of what somebody else wanted you to be. You were forced to do things that did not come naturally, went against your instincts, and did not mesh with your sense of purpose.

The highest order of occupation is finding work that is a total expression of who we are. Work that offers a nice paycheck, but no room for expressing the essence of who we are, is a disheartening compromise.

Do work that expresses who you are. Life is too short to live out someone else's picture of what you ought to be.

Dream Days

How much time is left to achieve your personal dreams? If you are 40-years-old and you plan on living until you are 80-years-old, you have a limited amount of time left with which you can achieve your dreams.

Of your 40 remaining years, you will sleep away 13 years. You will use another three years eating, growing, bathing, reading, etc.! You will use a year in transport. You have 23 years left.

Should you happen to be in a job that is not acting as a channel to your personal dream – and you plan on staying in that job – you just used up another 13 years.

You have ten years left.

Now, there are your family and friends, and you want to invest good time there. If you spend one to two hours a day interacting with your spouse, children, parents, and friends, you now have about seven years left. Seven years would be a lot of time to achieve some personal dreams if you could start today and not stop for the next seven years.

How quickly have the last seven years of your life gone by? We must appreciate every moment and every opportunity to pursue our personal dreams because, on this planet, the clock is always ticking.

Dream days come in hourly chunks of time. Use your dream days well.

The Real Contest

Is success a ladder to climb? Is success something to go out and get?

Not according to Henry Ford who believed success had more to do with giving than getting. He wrote:

"Success is not rare. It is common. Very few miss a measure of it. It is not a matter of luck or contesting, for certainly no success can come from preventing the success of another. It is a matter of adjusting one's efforts to overcome obstacles and one's abilities to give the services needed by others. There is no other possible success. Most people think of it in terms of getting: success, however, begins in terms of giving."

Ford's words are much needed in our get-ahead society. I want to focus specifically on his statement that "no success can come from preventing the success of another."

Success is not a defensive act and does not come to defensive people. Protecting our turf, covering our backsides, and trying to keep others from claiming credit will not help us reach our potential. It is not the go-getters who truly get, but the "go-givers!"

Look for needs and then work fervently and heartily to meet those needs. Then, you will find yourself rising to new levels of success.

High Dives

Remember the first time you dove off the high dive? That was one of those moments where you proved yourself. In his book, *A Gift of Wings,* Richard Bach writes:

"Remember the high board at the swimming pool? After days of looking up at it you finally climbed the wet steps to the platform. From there, it was higher than ever. There were only two ways down: the steps to defeat or the dive to victory. You stood on the edge, shivering in the hot sun, deathly afraid. At last you leaned too far forward, it was too late for retreat, and you dived. The high board was conquered, and you spent the rest of the day diving. Climbing a thousand high boards, we demolish fear, and turn into human beings."

Every once in awhile, we encounter a new high dive in our lives. Are we just now climbing the stairs, or are we now on the board contemplating our leap?

If it is a risk you need to take, don't you dare look back! You are not going down those stairs. Get to the edge. Decide on a dive, a jump, or even a cannonball, but make your leap – you will never be the same.

Plateaus

How many times have you taken on a hobby, sport, or venture and given up out of frustration because you seemed to reach a plateau?

According to the classic motivational author, Dale Carnegie, we should not allow ourselves to be dissuaded by plateaus. In his book, *How to Develop Self-Confidence*, he wrote:

> *"We never learn anything - be it golf, a new language or public speaking - by means of gradual improvement. We advance by sudden jerks and abrupt starts. Then we may remain stationary for a few weeks, or even lose some of the proficiency we have gained. Psychologists call these periods of stagnation, 'plateaus in the curve of learning.' We may strive hard for a long time and not be able to get off one of these 'plateaus' and onto an upward ascent again.*
>
> *Some people, not realizing this curious fact about the way we progress, get discouraged on these plateaus and abandon all effort. This is extremely regrettable, for if they were to persist, if they were to keep on practicing, they would suddenly find that they had lifted like the airplane and make tremendous progress again."*

Carnegie had an interesting perspective on progress. Success does not come gradually; it comes in sudden stops and starts. What is most important is that we keep ourselves on the learning curve.

Wish Upon a Star

When you were a child, do you remember that secret thrilling moment at your birthday party just before you blew out the candles and made a wish? And, you knew if you told anyone, your wish would not come to pass.

I remember dropping a penny in a wishing well. I also remember the times Mom made chicken and we all fought for the wishbone.

It is sad that by the time many become adults they have discontinued the wishing process. They are so out of breath that they can no longer blow out the candles. They are unable to find a spare penny, and they stopped fighting for the wishbone long ago.

Why? For many, their dreams were dashed and their hopes were shattered. But without dreams, hopes, and wishes, life is a dull, gray canvas with nothing to look forward to.

There is a child within each of us that wants to keep wishing because, "You just never know!"

You never get too old for wishing. The next time you blow out the candles or look upon the stars, put your cynicism aside. Renew your hopes and make a wish – but don't tell anyone what you wished for.

Dragons

Mapmakers in medieval times faced a real problem. They were given the job of charting the continent, but were not exactly well traveled themselves. So when they came to a border they had not crossed, they drew fire-breathing dragons toward their own country's boundaries.

These maps, when viewed by the common masses, caused people to believe that, if they crossed the border, these infernal beasts would consume them. Needless to say, travel agents were having a tough go of it.

Being fully enlightened today, we know there are no dragons to fear. Yet the great majority of the masses never cross their own restricting borders.

Many people when challenged to go to new places, try new things, or try doing things in a different way, simply refuse. When asked, "Why not?" they respond, "I don't know, I just don't want to."

We need to try new ventures, stretch our abilities, and give more than we do. Each of us has the ability to test our endurance a bit further. Without taking risks, we settle into the quicksand of complacency.

Today, make the decision to cross a new border – unless, of course, you believe in dragons.

"Baby Steps"

In the movie, *What about Bob?,* Bill Murray gives an hilarious portrait of a neurotic trying to adjust to everyday life. Bob decides that he will confront his fears by taking the walk of life in "baby steps."

When we are done laughing at this comic tale, we are left with the distinct impression that maybe "baby steps" are not such a bad idea.

When we try something new and challenging, we risk failure and discouragement. If we are too badly stung by the experience, we tend to shrink back and stop taking risks.

When we stop taking risks, we are done – the adventure is over. Consequently, it is sometimes best, in the realm of risk, to take it slow. Easy does it. One step at a time.

If we rush or leap without guidance on our road to risk, we might end up in a detour or stuck on a dead-end – which leads to discouragement.

If you are trying to muster up the courage to "jump off the high dive" in your life or career, remember that it is OK to walk to the end of the diving board in "baby steps."

Goals are Easier than They First Appear

John Wooden, the legendary basketball coach from UCLA, was known as the "Wizard of Westwood" – and with good reason.

He had the unusual ability to bring the best out in his players. One of his techniques with players having trouble at the free-throw line was to take them up on a stepladder to get a view above the rim.

He would then illustrate how large the goal was by having the player drop two basketballs through the hoop at one time, always surprising them that this was possible.

From below and under pressure, that rim can look awfully small. Coach Wooden knew that, to succeed, he first had to help change the players' perspectives. It worked and, immediately, their free-throw percentages improved.

The implications here are powerful. When goals and milestones we deem as too difficult intimidate us, we need a change of perspective.

Talk to those who have already done it and find out how they made it. Their view is from "above the rim" and they know that it was not nearly as difficult as it seemed from below the rim.

Reaching our goals, no matter how lofty, is sometimes simply a matter of changing our perspectives.

What Do You Know?

One of the keys to success in the next decade has been identified as "developing a specialized knowledge base."

It has been stated that if you were to study any given topic for five to ten minutes a day for two years, you would know more than 99 percent of the population on that topic. You would be an expert!

The knowledge it once took mankind 500 years to assimilate now takes about a month. Knowledge is multiplying at a runaway pace.

We are living in the Information Age, where only those with a student's attitude and a voracious appetite for learning can keep up.

A real key for succeeding in today's world is to have the openness and desire to learn. "Yearn to learn" if you want to forge ahead.

The question today is not, "What do you know?" Rather, the question is, "What don't you know?" and "What are you doing to learn it?"

If knowledge truly is power, then we all have access to unlimited power!

FULFILLING **YOUR** POTENTIAL

Falling Off Your Horse

Some years ago, I received a solicitation in the mail from an investment newsletter. Amazingly, their letter reported that their stock picks were up "an average of 72 percent!" I perused their list of stocks and noticed that, out of more than 50 stocks, not one had lost money.

The old adage, "If it looks too good to be true..." certainly comes to mind here. So does another adage, "Never trust a person who hasn't fallen off a horse at least 50 times."

Why is that? There is a lot of good that comes from falling off a horse. First, we realize we are human. Second, we realize we cannot always be in control. And, finally, we realize that no matter how hard we work and try to win, sometimes we lose anyway.

Some folks are so busy putting up a good front that they cannot admit when they fall on their rears.

It is easier to trust people who talk as easily about their losses as they do about their wins. The real winners are not those who never fall down, but those who know how to keep getting back up!

Win Without Bragging;
Lose Without Excuse

It seems that in much of today's athletic world, there are some games people are trying to win that have nothing to do with the game itself.

The idea of this game called, "trash talking," is to psychologically throw off your opponent through verbal harassment and intimidation.

I remember playing in a pickup basketball game last winter. The opponent I was guarding proceeded to tell me how great he was and what considerable damage he was going to do to me. I watched with slightly concealed glee as he missed his first eight shots and bounced the ball off of his feet.

Many of today's so-called "stars" promote this game of verbal one-upmanship. It is a scary trend when people mistake "talking about being good" with actually "being good."

The reality of competition is that, at the end, there is a score and the party that performed the best wins.

I prefer the credo I heard espoused by tennis great, Bjorn Borg, "When you win, win without bragging; when you lose, lose without excuse."

The Harder You Work, The More It Means

I watched a young man in our neighborhood ride a bike his parents had given to him. He jumped off the bike, threw it to the ground, and ran off to see his friends. Soon his bike had chipped paint, a bent sprocket – eventually, was useless.

The next bike, his parents made him pay for himself. He worked long and hard to save the money. This time, he carefully set the bike up on the kickstand, washed it regularly, and locked it up in public.

In light of this, it is amazing how many Americans swallow the Wall Street and Madison Avenue pitches that we are obligated to give our children everything we did not have – right on through to paying for all of their college education.

Booker T. Washington in his classic, *Up From Slavery*, stated, "Hard work should not be avoided but sought out because it is hard work that makes the soul honest."

There is no need to envy those who have come by things easily or without effort; they are not as rich as you are. For those who have had to work for their gains know that the harder you have to work for something, the better care you will give to it!

Rejection in the Garbage

Norm was at an all-time low. He took the pile of pages – his manuscript and life's passion – and threw it in the garbage. That was it. Forty-plus rejections from 40 different publishers were quite enough. He had seen his hopes raised and dashed one too many times.

His wife came into the room and was horrified to see his book in the garbage and went to pull it out.

He said, "I forbid you to take that out. I have had enough."

Ruth was troubled. She did not want to go against her husband's wishes; but neither did she want to see his life's work go to the landfill.

He had been rejected so many times, by so many people, that he had run out of energy.

Ruth decided to follow his wishes – sort of. She left the manuscript in the garbage can, but wrapped it up and sent it to one more publisher.

This publisher took notice. He had never before received a manuscript in a garbage container. He read her explanatory note and then the manuscript. He decided to publish. Little did he realize the manuscript would become one of the top-sellers of all time.

The author? Norman Vincent Peale.

The book? *The Power of Positive Thinking.*

The Mind Once Stretched

A sports physician once told me that a high percentage of athletic injuries are the result of not stretching first. The body is not limber, loose, and ready for impact and, therefore, suffers the consequences. "A few minutes spent stretching," he told me, "can save hours of agony."

The same rule seems to apply in the realm of thinking. Oliver Wendell Holmes said, "The mind, once stretched, can never again return to its original proportions."

A friend in the publishing business informed me that 90 percent of all books are read by less than ten percent of the population. That tells me that not enough people are being properly stretched.

People who have the attitude that they have a lot to learn know they can never learn enough.

Too often we enter the arena of new endeavors, challenges, and competition, and leave limping because we have not allowed our minds to be properly stretched.

Great books and literature abound in every arena. So, before you jump into the game, take the doctor's advice – take a few short minutes to get properly stretched!

Change Comes with Dissatisfaction

Clarence had been looking forward to this date for quite awhile. He and his favorite girl were going to paddle a boat out to the scenic little island for a picnic.

The trip was all he imagined. They rowed at a pleasant pace, beached the boat, and began to set up the lunch.

But Clarence's date noticed that he had forgotten the ice cream he promised. Good to his word and realizing his mistake, Clarence jumped back in the boat, paddled across the waterway, and brought back the ice cream.

By then, the sun was fully up and he was breaking out in a sweat. Even though his best shirt was no longer looking its best, Clarence, with grand chivalry, presented the ice cream.

"Oh, Clarence, thank you," she remarked, "but you forgot the topping."

Always the gentleman, he jumped back in the boat and rowed back and forth again. By now, he was dirty and exhausted – and extremely dissatisfied with the tedious process of rowing. He decided that there had to be a better way. From that day, Clarence Evinrude went to work developing that "better way" – the outboard motor.

Clarence's story illustrates that the best impetus for change is extreme dissatisfaction.

How can you creatively channel your dissatisfaction?

You Know You Are Right

I once saw a poster of a Mafia boss pointing his stocky finger and saying, "If I want your opinion, I'll give it to you."

Samuel Butler once said, "There is no mistake so great as that of always being right."

How many folks have you met who act like they know more than the *Encyclopedia Britannica;* who will argue with a stop sign; who must have the last word in every discussion and debate?

Samuel Butler points out that the more often we argue that we are right, the fewer the people who will want to hear what we have to say.

We Americans must love a good debate. How else could these political "verbal wrestling matches" continue to flourish on television where guests spend the entire half-hour interrupting one another and taking one-upmanship to the nth degree?

Once in awhile, it really pays to not be right; to make statements such as, "You know, you made a good point there," or "I never thought of that," or "I think you might be right."

Knowledge is great, but can lead to arrogance. Wisdom, on the other hand, is knowledge that has no need to flaunt itself and knows when to let the other person be right.

Great Spirits

Young Al was thrilled with the gift his father gave him – his very own compass.

His fascination with the object seemed way beyond that of the average eight-year-old. It wasn't just the fact that the mechanism told him North from South and East from West; what triggered Al's imagination was the fact that some invisible force in the universe – a magnetic polarity – caused the arrow to turn a certain direction.

Al figured that, if there is an invisible force affecting his compass, there must be other invisible forces as well – forces that affect us in ways we cannot see or imagine. This thought became the driving obsession in his life.

Many thought Al was a little strange. Some tried to discourage him from his searching and theorizing on things unseen. People told him to focus on things he could see; but he would not be dissuaded.

Little Al – Albert Einstein – later wrote, "Great Spirits have always encountered violent opposition from mediocre minds."

If you are suffering violent oppositions for your unusual ideas, remember that you are in good company.

The Knuckle-Ballers

I have always admired the ingenuity of the "knuckle-ballers. I am speaking of those major league pitchers who throw that softly floating baseball – too slow for any hitter to resist. Batters prepare themselves to knock it into the next universe, only to watch it drop out of sight and wink at them as it drops into the catcher's mitt. The knuckler makes great hitters look foolish.

It is not just the pitch that impresses me, but the pitcher. Many men have prolonged their careers by years, just by learning this pitch.

Hoyt Wilhelm pitched until he was 50! Imagine a 50-year-old out-crafting 22-year-old, carved from granite, muscle-bound, highly trained athletes! How did he do it? Not with speed, not with power, but with *finesse*. These sluggers who have no problem with a 98 mph fastball, cannot make contact with the elusive knuckler.

When other pitchers' arms are tired, their careers are over. But the knuckleballer's career is just beginning.

John Wooden said, "Do not let what you cannot do, interfere with what you can do."

If you would like to be more competitive with those who are younger and in better shape, do not think about quitting – think about learning a new pitch!

Where Is the Ladder Leaning?

Every once in awhile we need to stop whatever we are doing and ask ourselves, "Why am I doing this?" instead of, "What am I doing?" or "How am I doing?"

The question "why?" brings us to the core of our activity, which is purpose. If we do not stop now and then to ask this question, we can easily get caught up in the "activity trap" – where we do and do, but yet do not feel a sense of accomplishment about what we do.

The question is good for two reasons. First, if we have a positive sense about why we do what we do, we are reassured by the answer. And, second, if we are unsure about why we do what we do, we are forced to confront an issue in our lives that will only get larger if not confronted.

In his book, *7 Habits of Highly Effective People*, Steven Covey writes, "It is incredibly easy to get caught up in an Activity Trap, in the busyness of life, to work harder and harder at climbing the ladder of success only to discover it's leaning against the wrong wall."

Before you take one more step up the ladder, make sure it is leaning on the wall you want to climb.

Be Yourself

"Be yourself," the saying goes, "because no one else is better qualified." The following anonymous essay well illustrates this point:

"Ever since I was a little kid, I didn't want to be me. I wanted to be like Billy Widdledon, and Billy didn't even like me. I walked and talked like him. I signed up for what he signed up for. Which is why Billy Widdledon changed. He hung around Herby Vandeman; he began to walk and talk like Herby Vandeman. He mixed me up! I began to walk and talk like Billy Widdledon who was walking and talking like Herby Vandeman.

Then it dawned on me that Herby Vandeman walked and talked like Joey Haverlin who walked and talked like Corky Saginson. So here I am walking and talking like Billy Widdledon's imitation of Herby Vandeman's version of Joey Haverlin who's trying to walk and talk like Corky Sabinson. And who is Corky trying to imitate? Of all people, Dopey Wellington, the little pest who walks and talks like me!"

If your children ask you what you want them to be when they grow up, tell them, "I want you to grow up to be yourself."

Now, that is a real accomplishment!

"I Don't Do Windows"

As a motivational speaker, I'm often asked, "How do you motivate people?"

My answer, "I can't motivate anyone."

The word "motivate" comes from the Latin words "moti" and "vatum" which means, "Move yourself!"

The concept of motivation is well-illustrated by a story a friend told me:

"I was driving by some homeless men in a large city. The men held signs asking for work.

Being touched, I drove up to a man who held a sign which read, 'Will work for food.'

So, I opened my window and asked, 'Do you want work?'

'Yeah,' he answered. 'What is it?'

I answered, 'I need some windows cleaned at my home.'

The homeless man stared blankly at me and replied, 'I don't do windows.'

I was stunned as I drove off."

The man has no money and no food – but he doesn't do windows!

Motivation is simple. Motivation happens when you are so hungry that you will do what you have to do – no matter how humble – to get the job done.

Learning to Lose

Back in 1958, Frank and Dan Carney started operating a pizza parlor in Wichita to help pay for their college educations. Some 20 years later, Frank sold a chain of pizza restaurants called Pizza Hut for several hundred million dollars.

Carney's advice to those hoping to start a new venture is a little offbeat. He says that you have to learn to lose. He explains it this way:

> *"I've been involved in about 50 different business ventures and about 15 have worked. That means I have about a 30 percent average. But, you need to be at bat and it's even more important to be at bat after you lose. You never learn when you are winning. You need to learn to lose."*

Here is a man who admits to more than 35 business failures; but, more importantly, here is someone who has never stopped learning from his mistakes.

Henry C. Link said, "While one person hesitates because he feels inferior, the other is busy making mistakes and becoming superior!"

Nice Try

For more than eight years, the hopeful writer wrote short stories and articles for publication – and for more than eight years, they came back as rejections. He did not give up, however, and for that our society will always be grateful.

One day an editor sent him back an article, not with an acceptance, but with a little note that said, "Nice try."

That was it – just a short letter of encouragement to a very discouraged writer. The young writer was moved to tears and infused with new hope.

Finally, after many years of effort, he wrote a book that deeply affected our modern world. He titled the book, *Roots*.

Alex Haley, because of hope and persistence, went from obscurity to one of the most powerful writers of his day. It is interesting to note this root of *Roots*.

Edmund Burke said, "Never despair but if you do, work on, even in despair!"

Take Fun Seriously

One reason that many relationships, families, and organizations fail to succeed is that they "fail to take fun seriously."

Too often the parent or manager is guilty of growling, "OK, we've had enough fun, let's get back to work," – as if no productivity is possible in an air of humor.

Thomas Edison once received a letter from a solemn stockholder:

> "'A Vice-President of your company,' he wrote, 'doesn't have a proper sense of dignity of his position and of his association with you. I'm told sometimes his laugh can be heard through his door and all over the office.'
>
> Edison sent the letter to the Vice-President tied to the framed picture of a laughing, jolly friar. 'Hang this picture in the entrance hall,' he wrote, 'and have everyone in the office look at it. Let it be a constant reminder that good business is never done except in a reasonably goodhumored frame of mind and on a human basis.'"

Now, that is genius from one of the "greats."

True accomplishment and achievement is fun. Those who do not know how to have fun reminds me of the old-timer who told me, "Ever notice," he said, "about those folks that take themselves too seriously, that nobody else does?"

You've Got a Dream

How important is it to pursue your dreams? All important – if you ask those who have spent their lives with the regret of not having done so.

One young man had ambitions of becoming a professional golfer and excelled as an amateur in youth and college events. Upon graduation, his dad told him that it was time to settle down and get on with real life – and make money.

His dad invited him to join the successful family business, but the young man said he wanted to join the mini tour to see how good he could be.

His father, wanting to knock some sense into him, arranged for him to meet a wise and influential friend. This influential friend turned out to be the late Senator Hubert H. Humphrey.

When the Senator asked what the problem was, the young man explained his dilemma between golfing and entering the business world.

Humphrey stood up and exclaimed, "That's an easy choice! Go golf! If it is your dream, follow it!"

The young man told Humphrey, "I don't think that's what my father wanted me to hear!"

Humphrey then called his father and told him, "So few people even have a dream. When you meet someone who does, encourage it! Even if they fail, they're better off for trying!"

The Width and Depth

A friend of mine was trying to talk his elderly Norwegian aunt into taking a trip with him to Norway. Although she had always talked of going, when the opportunity actually came, she balked.

"What if the pipes freeze up in the house?" she fretted. "What if somebody robs the house?" and "Who will get my mail?"

On and on the excuses went. This resistance to risk was coming from a woman who always ate the right foods, was careful at all times, and took her vitamins. She had lived a long life, but a narrow one.

I once met relatives, in their 80s, who had never tasted pizza because they did not want to risk getting away from meat and potatoes. They also had never felt, seen, nor heard the wonder of the ocean's tide.

"I can't," they would say, or "I'd better not."

Louis Nizer said, "Although we cannot control the length of our lives, we can control the width and depth."

Risk and adventure add width and depth to our lives. After all, what good is a long journey if it is in a cul-de-sac where the view never changes?

"*Try*umph!"

In his book, *Steps to the Top*, Zig Ziglar writes about a Professor of Economics who gave a test to his class with three categories of questions, and instructed his students to choose one question from each section.

The first category was the most difficult and was worth 50 points. The second category, which was not as difficult, was worth 40 points. The third category, being the easiest, was worth only 30 points.

When the papers were returned, the students who had chosen the hardest questions were given "As." Those who chose 40-point questions were given "Bs." Those who chose the easy questions were given "Cs."

The students were confused, so they asked the professor how he graded the exam.

The professor smiled and responded, "I wasn't testing your knowledge, I was testing your aim!"

Great leaders have the ability to motivate people to reach higher than they think is possible. The person who accomplishes half of a 100-mile journey travels farther than the one who completes a ten-mile journey.

To go high, we must reach higher!

Browning said, "A man's reach should exceed his grasp or what's a heaven for?"

The true meaning of the word "triumph" can be found in the first syllable – "*try*umph."

The Good Old Days

While it is wonderful to look with anticipation at our tomorrows, and with fondness at our yesterdays, it is not good to focus forward or backward at the expense of the present.

Today is the "good old days" we will be talking about someday with our great-grandchildren. We need to begin to see it that way.

As a youth, I remember a neighbor who vividly talked about the Great Depression and World War II. He would say, "Don't tell me about the 'good old days.' Today is just great for me! I don't have to wait in line for a bowl of soup anymore, and I can have two bowls if I want. And, I don't have to watch loved ones go off and fight in wars."

Art Buchwald stated:

> *"We seem to be going through a period of nostalgia, and everyone seems to think yesterday was better than today. I don't think it was, and I would advise you not to wait ten years before admitting today was great. If you're hung up on nostalgia, pretend today is yesterday and just go out and have one heck of a time."*

Look around you. Enjoy the people and opportunities you meet. This is the yesterday you will one day remember.

Make Your Breaks

"I just need to catch a break!" are very dangerous words.

While it is true that many have become successful in various fields by being at the right place at the right time, or by knowing the right person, it is their skill and work ethic that caused them to get noticed.

An obvious and common element in reading the biographies of successful people is that they worked long and hard for their "breaks."

As one entertainer explains, "It takes a long time to become an overnight success!"

A cynic once noted, "The race does not always go to the swift, but that is the way to bet."

You win a race because you prepare for it.

William Holl stated, "You can do it gradually day by day and play by play if you WANT to do it, if you WILL to do it, if you WORK to do it over a sufficiently long period of time."

Are you waiting for a break? If so, you'd better heed Gibbon's words, "The winds and the waves are always on the side of the ablest navigators."

Ask the Right Person

The adage, "You'll never learn if you don't ask!" is a familiar phrase from our youth. But is there more to it than that?

A story is told about a father and his small son who were out walking one afternoon when the youngster asked how electricity went through the wires stretched between the telephone poles.

"Don't know," said the father. "I never knew much about the electricity."

A few blocks farther on, the boy asked what caused lightening and thunder.

"To tell you the truth," said the father, "I never exactly understood that myself."

The boy continued the questions throughout the walk – none of which his father could explain.

Finally, as they were nearing home, the boy asked, "Pop, I hope you don't mind my asking so many questions."

"Of course not," he replied. "How else are you going to learn?"

Sometimes we ask the right questions, but we ask the wrong people – and their answers may not help. So it often is with the advice of family or friends.

A key to asking good questions is to ask a person who, more than likely, knows the answers you need to hear.

Afraid to Ask

Any kid growing up who had this experience would never forget it. They ask a question, and their classmates laugh. Or, worse yet, the teacher laughs. What do they learn?

• Whatever you do, don't look stupid.
• Pretend to know when you don't.
• If you don't know, don't ask.

This defensive attitude will become a serious disability in our adult lives and careers. As stated by David Meier of the Center for Accelerated Learning, "Learning is no longer preparation for the job. It is the job!"

According to a Danish Proverb, "He who is afraid to ask is ashamed of learning."

The learning curve we all must face in our lives and careers is getting steeper every day. To stay ahead, we must begin learning that you cannot learn if you do not ask, and you must risk something to learn.

One corporate executive said, "Our ability to learn faster may be our only competitive advantage."

Today, it is not those asking questions that are being laughed at, but those who fail to ask.

A modern secret for becoming smart is to be willing to play stupid – at least for the moment.

You Deserve Better

There is probably no philosophical lament more common in our world than, "Life isn't fair."

We hear people saying of a kind individual, "She deserves better," or of a not-so-kind person, "I hope he gets what he deserves."

Many people treat life as if there should be some grand manager walking around handing out merit badges, financial rewards, and promotions on the basis of "being a good person."

This is not to say that sooner or later the laws of reciprocity will kick in and we will eventually "reap what we sow." "What goes around comes around" is a phrase often used to express this sentiment.

In the large scheme, however, people do *not* get what they deserve, but they get what they ask for and set out to attain. You may well deserve a raise, but what are the odds of getting one if you do not ask? The rewards you desire will not come passively. You must pursue, attain, plan, and ask.

Why should you become more aggressive and start attaining the things you want? Because you *deserve* better.

Programmed to Succeed

Back in 1983, the Australian sailing team stunned the sailing world by winning the America's Cup for the first time.

When the coach of the team was interviewed about the victory, he explained that he had read the book, *Jonathon Livingston Seagull,* and it had inspired him to make a cassette tape of the Australian team beating the American team. He had recorded a narration of the winning race over the sound effects of a sailboat cutting through the water.

He gave a copy of the tape to each member of the team, and asked them to listen twice a day for three years – which is 2,190 times!

Before they actually set sail in San Diego Harbor, in their minds they had already won that race 2,190 times. The fire of belief was burning brightly inside every member of that team.

Our potential and performance hinge on the quality of our beliefs about ourselves. Our minds work much like a computer – you do not program a champion with images of failure and words of resignation.

Rather, if you want to succeed, you must first believe you can and then begin the process of programming yourself with the sound effects of winning.

Delayed Gratification

Just how smart is your heart? The answer to that question just might be the key to your success.

In his book, *Emotional Intelligence*, author Daniel Goleman shares the emotional cornerstones that must be in place for us to make the most of our lives. Those who are well-developed in those areas are more likely to succeed.

One of those cornerstones is "The ability to delay impulse and gratification."

Consumer debt and personal bankruptcies are at all-time highs in our world for one primary reason: people do not know how to control their impulses to buy. Without the ability to delay gratification, they cannot achieve financial security or success.

For example, you are driving down the road and someone cuts you off. You want to chase them down or offer an infamous gesture, but you *don't,* because you are in control.

All your neighbors are buying new trucks. You see one you like, but your budget is already tight, so you decide to delay gratification and drive your beater for one more year.

The impulses we fail to control will come back to haunt us. The gratification we fail to delay will bring unwanted stress into our lives.

According to Goleman, those who can control their emotional impulses will better control their destinies because their smarts come from their heart.

Recognizing Ability

In an interview, a champion bodybuilder was asked how he got started.

He answered, "I was walking by a gym one day and a man working out there saw me walk by and said, 'You should be a bodybuilder, you could be great.'"

He was right.

A manager for a company was talking to a young man tending bar. He told him, "You could be quite successful in sales."

Little did he know that he would someday become one of the best in the nation for that company.

These people had the ability to see ability. They saw potential in people who did not see it in themselves.

People often underestimate themselves. They settle for a station in life far below their potential. Often, the impetus they need *can* and *is* provided by someone else who *recognizes* their abilities. Suddenly they view themselves differently and their lives begin to change.

Elbert Hubbard put it this way: "There is something that is much more scarce, something far finer, something rarer than ability. It is the ability to recognize ability."

Those that Care the Least

Herb Cohen is a master negotiator. For years he has been training people on the proper way to negotiate. He says that negotiation affects all of our relationships – business and personal. We negotiate with our spouses, children, and co-workers.

Cohen says that one of the great psychological keys to being a successful negotiator is: "They that seem to care the least have the most to gain."

In other words, the more desperate you posture yourself, the higher the price you will pay.

The more stress you put upon yourself to get what you want, the less chance you have of obtaining it. When people see your stress, anxiety, desperation, and inflexibility, they know that they are in control and will begin to take advantage of you.

Too often it is the desperate individual who gets exploited. If this has happened to you, remember next time to:

- Act as if you can live with either outcome.
- Refuse to put pressure on yourself to get your way.
- Relax, and be ready to get up and walk away at least for the time being.

For as Cohen puts it, "The more you really want something, the less you can afford to really show it."

Write It Down

It is always interesting to hear success stories.

Steve Lorry writes about Scot Adams who worked in the corporate world for 17 years – all the while dreaming of being a cartoonist.

He finally decided to start a new practice of writing down his goal – "I will become a syndicated cartoonist" – 15 times a day!

Not long after he began writing his goal, he sent his *Dilbert* doodles to numerous syndicates. He received many rejections, but eventually received the one acceptance he wanted.

His *Dilbert* comic strip now appears in hundreds of papers and has drawn a national cult following. In addition, his first book, *The Dilbert Principle*, has already sold nearly a million copies.

Adams says, at first he laughed cynically at the idea of writing down goals and creating a better future. He toyed with the idea, however, and the first goal came to pass, and then another. He got serious about his goal writing, and now it is a habit he will never break.

And what is Scot's next goal? He has already written, "I will win a Pulitzer Prize."

For those who have time to doodle, start writing down your goals – it provides a much better map for your future!

Your Reference Group

"You are as good as the company you keep." As a youth, I remember hearing that phrase from adults concerned that I make the right associations.

As an adult, I now realize that peer pressure is not an exclusive phenomenon of adolescence, but one that follows us our entire lives.

The associations we keep profoundly affect our character, levels of achievement, and attitudes toward life.

Harvard studied the factors leading to business success. They found that at the top of the list was an individual's "reference group." This group includes those individuals you seek to associate with or relate most to.

The study demonstrated that people rarely, if ever, achieve beyond the level of their reference group. This group exercises an unspoken influence over what people will attempt to achieve or believe to be possible.

Just as bad company corrupts good manners, good company catapults you past bad patterns.

The quickest way to gauge what you think of yourself is to take a good look at the company you keep.

Easy to Fail

It has been said that, "95 out of 100 people do not achieve anything of significance in their lives simply because it is easier to fail, or just coast along, than it is to live up to one's potential."

Someone else said, "Most people are as lazy as they dare to be – and still get by."

There is an element of truth in both statements, indicating that, somewhere along the way, many have grasped the wrong definitions of failure and success. For example, success should not be defined as "Doing as little as possible, and still getting a paycheck."

Napoleon Hill defined success as, "The progressive realization of a worthy ideal."

Progress equals success – if the cause or ideal is worthy.

A failure was once defined as "Someone who has the talent or ability to accomplish much more than they have."

Failure is a lack of progress whether motivated by laziness or fear.

It is important to keep making progress; for although it may be easier to fail, it is certainly harder to live with.

Declare Your Intentions

There is something about verbalizing a thought that brings it to life.

An idea, intention, or goal can lie dormant in the storehouse of your mind. Once you articulate your intention, you plant it into the soil of possibilities.

Be careful to whom you declare your intentions, however. Choose positive people – for we can all use a little help. And, remember...

- Fantasies can become realities, once verbalized.
- Ideas need to be articulated to be improved upon.
- Great emotional power is released when we declare our intentions to another positive individual.

Even so, be prepared for negative reactions from those who will resist or resent your goals. Some people will view you as a threat; and others, as an idealist. Some will even laugh at you. If you can survive their reactions, you will be able to survive any adversity.

You will release an incredible creative power when you speak out. Declare your intentions positively – with enthusiasm and integrity.

Say what you mean, and mean what you say. And, remember, most people do not carry out their intentions until they declare their intentions.

The Need to Think

At first, the 90-minute commute each way to work bothered me. I had to get up extra early and fight traffic, and I would often arrive home exhausted. To occupy myself, I tried every radio station on the dial.

Then one day, I decided to try something different: I would just use the time to think. The more I practiced "just thinking" on my drive, the more I saw how badly I needed the practice. I realized that...

1. I make too many decisions without enough thought.
2. I speak too many words without considering the consequences.
3. I spend too much time doing, and not enough time thinking about what I am doing.

When we treat thinking like a seven-course meal instead of a quick snack between appointments, we recognize the need to:

1. Take *inventory* of our thoughts (we harbor many thoughts that are ill-motivated and misdirected).
2. Take *charge* of our thoughts (we harbor many thoughts that are self-defeating, self-sabotaging, and fatalistic).

In a modern world where we think of "doing it alone" as real living, we need to be reminded of Cicero's words, "To think is to live."

Correct and Adjust

Exactly how does someone navigate a trip to the moon? You would think that, with all the brilliant minds at NASA, they would simply chart a straight course from here to there – you know, draw a line from A to B!

Well, it is not that easy. Ponder this interesting fact from the world of space travel: the space shuttle, with all its power, spends only about three percent of its time on a true course to its goal, and the other 97 percent of its time simply adjusting and correcting its course.

Amazing stuff. Sort of makes me feel a little better about the path I have taken to some of my goals.

You would think you could just draw a straight line from A to B in your life as well, but it never seems to work out that easily. There are many distractions, adverse conditions, and general things to do. It is a wonder we even spend three percent of our time on a true course.

It is not just setting a lofty goal that helps us to achieve, but having the discipline needed (97 percent of the time) to keep our hands at the controls and eyes on the course.

If you want to reach the moon, you have to be willing to spend most of your time correcting and adjusting.

FULFILLING **YOUR** POTENTIAL

Big Dogs

FULFILLING **YOUR** POTENTIAL

Travis was smaller – and I mean significantly smaller – than all the other players on my 8th grade baseball team.

From the first practice, however, I saw something special in Travis – real heart. When others loafed, he hustled. When others laughed, he worked.

All year he begged to play shortstop and, every time he asked, his teammates would laugh and say things like, "You're too short – a ground ball would go over your head!"

What these players did not know was that I was going to give Travis his chance. Even though I stand 6', my father is only about 5'6". He was once the runt of the ball field. Everyone told him he was too short – all the way into semi-pro ball!

The last day of the season we were playing for the championship. In the last inning, we were up by one and I told Travis to go out and play shortstop. The team looked at me like I was crazy.

Soon the bases were loaded with just one out, and it looked like our lead would soon slip away. The batter hit a line shot up the middle and Travis dove as far as his small frame would allow, and made the catch! He jumped up and tagged a runner – an unassisted double play. His teammates mobbed him.

A big heart can always overcome a small body or, as my dad liked to say, "It ain't the size of the dog in the fight, but the size of the fight in the dog."

Brilliant Mind – Broken Body

Steven Hawking is widely regarded as the most brilliant physicist since Albert Einstein. He holds the prestigious Newton's Chair of Mathematics at Cambridge University.

Hawking has become a master communicator for a field which has become so technical that only a very small number of specialists are able to master the mathematics used to describe the complex concepts.

Hawking believes that the basic ideas about our origin and universe can be communicated in a way that lay people can understand. He accomplished this feat in his great book, *A Brief History of Time.*

The irony of this brilliant mind and communicator is that he has been bound to a wheelchair for the last 30 years by ALS (Lou Gehrig's Disease) and must use a keyboard, operated by a speech synthesizer, to speak – for he has no voice of his own.

Hawking never resigned because of his disability. In fact, he claims that the disability has helped him to become a better communicator.

What is Hawking's real genius? The genius of courage to focus only on the good that can come out of an otherwise horrible condition. Now, that is pure genius!

Define Your Destiny

What is your purpose? I am not asking "what" you are doing; I am asking "why" you are doing what you are doing. What is your reason for being?

The reason I ask is that, if you do not have a sense of purpose driving what you do, soon you will not enjoy whatever it is you are doing and you will stop doing it as well as you can.

At some point in our lives, we must stop and define our destinies. We must assess and decide what we want to accomplish with our lives.

Defining our destinies is different from defining our occupations. For example, some will become doctors to help others, and others will become doctors to help themselves.

Defining our destinies is about establishing the impact we choose to have on others while on this earth.

This book is the tangible result of my introspection. When I "defined my destiny," I wrote, "I will encourage people to lead more positive lives." It is my hope that you will be encouraged by these words.

Defining your destiny takes your life from the realm of random roaming to a place of impact and purpose!

Where Creativity Lies

John F. Welch, Jr., in a speech to future business leaders, said, "We know where most of the creativity, the innovation, the stuff that drives productivity lies - in the minds of those closest to the work."

The greatest ideas and innovations do not proceed from the ivory towers. Too many organizations in our world rely on the creativity of people who are too far removed from the world they are leading.

It is risky to sit in a plush corner office, behind a golden nameplate for 10 or 20 years, as it leads to offering the same answers for situations that changed long ago. The wise organization realizes wisdom lies on the front lines.

Years ago, I read about engineers and architects who were stumped about where to put an elevator in a building. A janitor overheard them talking and suggested placing it outside the building and giving it glass walls.

They all laughed and scoffed at the suggestion – save one architect. He sensed that the janitor was right.

Perhaps you have been in a hotel or building that has such an elevator.

Innovation lies on the front lines. If you want an answer, go to those closest to the action!

A View From the Ridge

Morris West in his book, *A View from the Ridge,* writes:

"Ask anyone who has survived a cardiac event and they'll tell you the same thing: every hour of every day is a bonus. You prize people. You understand that they can be as fragile and fearful as you have been. You don't quarrel anymore; you discuss. And you don't grasp at things, because after all, the Creator didn't close his hand on you but let you sit quietly, like a butterfly, on his palm.

When you read accounts like this one from Morris West, you realize that some of the best lessons for life come from those who have come closest to losing it. Then, and only then, do they appreciate what they have. These individuals realize the importance of:

- Being grateful for every day.
- Understanding that everyone has weaknesses.
- Listening, rather than arguing.
- Refusing to lead lives of "quiet desperation"
  (as Thoreau put it), controlled by greed and envy.

Some of the greatest views on this planet come from standing on the very edge.

See the Big Picture

A group of co-workers began to squabble and fight. They disagreed over strategies and who was responsible for what. Their disagreements erupted at a meeting; hostilities aired and tempers flared.

The team spirit was broken over the little details they could not agree upon. It was about miscommunication, lack of respect, and a failure to listen to one another.

After the blowout, someone asked what brought them together in the first place. It all started with a noble goal – a dream to build a company that would improve the quality of life.

They had lost sight of the goal and had forgotten the big picture.

This company was like a relay race team stopping to argue in the middle of the race. While they argued, competitors breezed on by.

The reason for entering a race is to reach the goal – hopefully, before anyone else.

When dissatisfied or angry, it is important to occasionally step back and see the big picture.

FULFILLING **YOUR** POTENTIAL

Astound Yourself

Have you come close to reaching your potential? Have you pressed yourself to the very limits of your abilities? How many people can answer a truthful "yes" to these questions?

Why do we take such vicarious pleasure in watching events like the Olympics? Is it just to see victory? No. It is to see athletes who have sacrificed all and given all to be there – laying everything they are and have on the line, in front of a world stage. These athletes put out like there is no tomorrow, and we all love to see this kind of effort.

Thomas Edison put it this way, "If we did all the things we are capable of doing, we would literally astound ourselves."

All of us are capable of doing so much more – we are nowhere near tapping our full potential. The greatest barriers that exist are those we allow to exist.

Decide to go and astound yourself!

Energy vs. Talent

As a youth, I was in love with the game of basketball. It became quite apparent to me early on that I would have to make up in desire what I lacked in natural talent. There were players that could run faster and jumper higher than I could, so I put my emphasis on working harder.

After my team won a city championship, the coach gathered the team together to congratulate us. He said he had decided to give an individual award, the "Mr. Hustle" Award. I flushed with proud embarrassment as he called my name.

The lesson was not lost on me. He had not given any "Mr. Talent" or MVP awards; rather, he rewarded desire. Diving after loose balls had paid off.

Jeffrey Archer wrote:

> *"Never be frightened by those you assume have more talent than you do, because in the end energy will prevail. My formula is: energy plus talent and you are a king; energy and no talent and you are a prince; talent and no energy and you are a pauper."*

Even with little or no talent, we all can be princes if we have king-sized hearts.

Reward Improvement

Steve Young, one of the greatest quarterbacks to ever play in the NFL, improved throughout his entire career. For years he backed up one of the all-time greats, Joe Montana. Once given a shot, he proved that he, too, could dominate the game and lead his team to championships.

Young understood the need to constantly improve, and also the need to learn how to better teach this principle:

> *"I wish parents would understand that if their child drops eight fly balls one day and then only drops six the next, that's a reason to go to Dairy Queen. The principle thing is competing against yourself. It's about self-improvement, about being better than you were the day before."*

Steve Young is right. We too often put the spotlight on perfection instead of improvement. We reward zero errors instead of fewer errors.

This approach zaps the "want to" out of a lot of would-be achievers who give up because they know they can never be perfect.

When we focus on improvement and rewards, people will improve.

"What Do You Do?"

When I meet people, I always know "the question" will come up. I do not know why, but I have always hated answering. The question they inevitably ask is, "So, what do you do?"

"What do you do?"

An individual's answer to this question seems to be the American definition of who a person is. "I'm a lawyer." "I'm a teacher." "I'm a plumber." "I'm a preacher."

Once you answer this question, that is all they really need to know about you.

For this one-dimensionality, we can only blame ourselves. When children are very young, we start asking, "What do you want to be when you grow up?" Right off the bat, we imply that there is only one road they can choose to express all their desires, dreams, creativity, and curiosity.

Yet, so many people find themselves unfulfilled in their work. Oftentimes, they take much more pleasure in their hobbies. We should teach youths to try to make their hobbies their work. We ought to ask, "How many things do you want to do when you grow up?"

What do I do? Everything I can. What do I want to be when I grow up? Every dream inside of me.

Malek's Law

Have you ever heard the saying, "By purposely reducing complexities, one increases ameliorating value?" Most likely not.

You are probably more familiar with the saying, "Simpler is better." Although most of us would probably agree with this saying, too often we stray from it. Society seems to have fallen victim to Malek's Law, which is, "Any simple idea will be worded in the most complicated way."

Malek's Law works hand in hand with Gumidge's Law, which states:

> *"The amount of expertise varies in inverse proportion to the number of statements understood by the general public." Which is really saying that, "If you keep people confused they'll think you're an expert."*

The need for simplicity is aptly illustrated by the runaway success of the book, *Men are from Mars, Women are from Venus,* which taught us that "men and women are different." Wow!

Good communication is not taking something simple and making it sound complex. Rather, it is taking something detailed and complex and boiling it down to its basic elements in a language everyone can understand.

We should be more impressed by those who help us to understand than by those who confuse us by too much learning.

Walk Like a Baby

"Joe is such a baby," his co-worker alleged. "He tries something and, if it doesn't work, he quits."

"Joe's not acting like a baby," I countered. "As a matter of fact, Joe would be better off if he *did* act like a baby! Joe is acting like an adult."

If you want a quick course in achievement and success, watch a baby learning to walk. Babies follow a very simple and, I might add, instinctive formula: They try, they fall down, they cry, they get back up, and they try again.

Now contrast this formula with typical adults taking their "first steps" in a new venture: They try, they fall down, they blame someone or something, they analyze why they fell, and they conclude that walking just wasn't meant for them.

So you see, Joe was busy acting like an adult. He should have had himself a good cry, picked himself up, and moved on.

Adults complicate things. Yet success is very simple; it boils down to persistence. Walk, fall, cry, get up, and try again.

If you want to go far, you will have to learn to walk just like a baby!

Sweet Smell of Success

Anthony Raissen has made millions because of his bad breath. No, people are not paying him to stay away from them or to breathe in another direction.

Raissen's breath was so bad, however, that he was no laughing matter. He says his breath was so bad that it almost ruined his marriage. Although he adored his wife, he also loved spicy foods.

He tried mints, gums, candies, and even parsley (but couldn't stomach the aftertaste). He was determined to find a cure.

In South Africa, he met chemists who had developed a mixture of parsley seed oil and sunflower oil that worked like a charm.

Raissen invested all he had in the formula and started a company called Breath Assure. He figured he was not alone in his battle with bad breath. Even though it worked, retailers would not even look at the unproved product.

Raissen and his wife decided to rollout their breath mints at a garlic festival in Southern California. By the end of the festival they knew they had hit a home run. They decided to market straight to consumers.

It is amazing how some creative people can turn a personal problem into a personal fortune. Raissen's desire to find a solution for his own bad breath turned into the sweet smell of success.

Adventures

Dr. Allan Zimmerman tells the story of Florence who, at age 82, took his course on change and risk-taking.

When he asked her what she wanted to learn to do for a risk at this stage of life, she said that she wanted to learn to drive an 18-wheeler!

Florence was slight of build – maybe 90 pounds – used a cane to walk, and looked a bit frail. Florence told the class that she wanted to put some "extra adventure into her life."

Several months later, Dr. Zimmerman received a letter from Florence. She had sent him a newspaper clipping about her amazing story – she had succeed in completing a vocational course on 18-wheelers and now is driving a semi across the country!

Amazingly, this was a goal she decided to act on at 82-years-old. And who said, "Adventures were just for kids?"

Florence is one of those rare individuals who understands the need to stay young and excited about life – and, occasionally, stray out of those comfort zones.

The next time you find yourself backing down from a risk-taking venture, think of Florence and then see if you can come up with one good reason you can't.

You Have to Know Who Knows

"If you want to see people acting like they know more than they really do, watch those who just got promoted."

These words were from a business manager who told me how he loathed people pretending to know things they didn't.

"Too often people make the mistake," he told me, "of believing the titles on their doors. When I got this job, I didn't have a clue as to how to do it. It was my past performance and potential that got me this promotion – not my vast sums of knowledge of the position I was entering."

"In an effort to look good," he continued, "we pretend to know things that we know nothing about."

This wise manager called his staff together and informed them that, although he was glad to have the job, he did not know the half of what he needed to do it well. He told them that he needed their help to learn to do his job well. Then he shut up and listened.

He was wise enough to realize that you do not need to know everything to succeed – you just have to know someone who does know!

TIME-Tested

Values

True North

Best-selling author Steven Covey has an interesting exercise he takes his audiences through to illustrate how wrong people can be, regardless of how right they think they are.

He asks the audience to close their eyes and to point to the North. He then asks them to open their eyes and observe where everyone is pointing. Without exception, people are pointing in every possible direction. The rest of his dialogue goes like this:

> "Now, let's go to the experts. All those who are absolutely confident you know which way North is, raise your hands!" (About 10 percent usually respond.) "Those with their hands up, please stand up. Now, those who are standing, close your eyes and point North. Now, open your eyes." (Again people are pointing in all possible directions)."And these are people who are absolutely sure they know which way is North."
>
> Covey concludes by saying, "If you're off by only one degree between here and Jerusalem, you'll end up in Moscow."

Perhaps you know or work with such "experts" who always claim to know where "true North" is. In actuality, "true North" cannot be found by one person all the time – it must be a team process.

It is far too easy for individuals, no matter how right they think they are, to point others in the wrong direction.

Good Leaders

Byrd Baggett once said, "Good leaders are like baseball umpires. They go practically unnoticed when they do their jobs right."

In an age where there are a thousand different definitions of what leadership is, I believe Baggett's quote defines it best – *leadership is doing!* A leader is not the one who sounds the siren – a leader is the one who puts out the fire. Like umpires, leaders ought to:

- Do their jobs the best they can.
- Not clamor for recognition.
- Settle disputes, not raise them.
- Stay out of the way of what others do best.

Too many so-called leaders want recognition – and often for what others have done. If you, too, start clamoring for recognition, you could fall with them into the self-aggrandizement trap.

In any group, people know who the individuals are that get the job done. These individuals are the backbone of the organization. They do not seek glory; instead, they seek to give the recognition to others who are working hard.

Contrary to popularly belief, good leadership does not always necessitate leading; sometimes it just means staying out of the way!

Glasses and Water

It seems to me that the age-old argument between the pessimists and optimists concerning the glass of water that is either half-empty or half-full will never end.

I have talked to enough people to know that there are more than just two views on that glass of water.

There are those cynics who say, "Who cares? The water is probably undrinkable anyway."

There are also the realists who say, "We'd better ration that water because it won't last forever."

My favorite view, however, is the grateful individual who said, "I'm just happy to have some water and a glass from which to drink – what a bonus!"

In a world that relentlessly promotes discontent, an attitude of gratitude stands out like a UFO. When we stop to think, we all have plenty to be thankful for in our lives. The things we do not have should never be allowed to rob us of the pleasure of the things we do have. Half of something is better than all of nothing.

So, who is right: the pessimist or the optimist? I do not know. But I do know this: to the person who is thirsty, any glass of water – half-empty or half-full – will do.

Anticipation / Realization

I have heard many highly successful individuals say, "One thing is for sure, the anticipation was certainly better than the realization."

I am not sure that any of these individuals regretted their success; but they did come to realize that "arriving" is not always the thrill it is cut out to be, and that greater joy and fulfillment comes from the path leading there.

The problem many of us face is that we have put so much emphasis on getting things done that we have nothing but stress and pressure along the way.

When Roger Maris broke Babe Ruth's single-season home run record of 60, it should have been the greatest thrill in his athletic career; however, he said that it was a great relief just to get it over with because of all the strain.

Milestones alone cannot satisfy. The human soul needs to know that the price paid to get there was not greater than the reward at the end.

In order to enjoy the milestones we reach in our lives, we need to learn how to enjoy the journey as much as the arrival.

You Cannot Fake Sincerity

I remember hearing one of Murphy's Laws, "The key to success is sincerity, if you can fake that you have it made!"

Recently, I was in line to buy an item at a discount store. "How are you today?" the checker asked, flashing a big smile.

"Great, just great," I answered, somewhat taken aback.

I was more accustomed to hearing clerks deliver a rote, hospitable quote like, "How are you?" or "Have a good day," or "Thank you for shopping at Any-Mart." I had stopped paying attention to their "greetings" a long time ago because their words were usually delivered by an expressionless face and a monotone voice.

It is amazing the amount of energy true sincerity brings to the simplest of greetings or the most routine encounters. Now, when I go to that store, I purposely look for the lane of that particular checker.

Murphy was right. The key to success is sincerity; but it cannot be faked. For it is not what you say that counts, but what you mean!

Taking Time

"I don't have time!" seems to be on the lips of everyone these days. Even the young seem to have more to do than ever. Wherever you go, people are busy.

What are the positive outcomes of all the hurrying and scurrying? In our efforts to make the most of our time, we need to take time to do the things that matter the most.

A classic piece titled, "Take Time," says it well:

Take time to work,
*   it is the price of success.*
Take time to think,
*   it is the source of power.*
Take time to play,
*   it is the secret of perpetual youth.*
Take time to read,
*   it is the fountain of wisdom.*
Take time to worship,
*   it is the highway to reverence.*
Take time to be friendly,
*   it is the road to happiness.*
Take time to laugh,
*   it is the music of the soul.*
Take time to dream,
*   it is hitching your wagon to a star.*

Next time you are doing your time management work, remember the one important thing in your schedule: *Make sure you take time to live!*

Ben Franklin's Simple Formula

The wisest of people seem to live by the simplest of rules.

Ben Franklin had a very simple formula for sorting out life's toughest decisions. When approaching any decision, Franklin would put two columns on a piece of paper marked "Advantages" and "Disadvantages."

In the "Advantages" column, he would list all the benefits and positive results he would receive if he went forward with his decision.

In the "Disadvantages" column, he would list all the drawbacks and potential consequences of his decision.

He then would study the impact of both. If, in his opinion, the advantages outweighed the disadvantages – and he felt he could live with the consequences as well as the positive benefits – he would go forward with his decision.

Good decisions were not foreign to the life of Franklin. He led a great life, filled with great choices determined by a simple formula.

Although the ways of society and survival become more complex, the rules of wisdom and success have always been just plain and simple.

Overnight Success

Alan Breed became an overnight success – and it took him only three decades to do it!

Over 35 years ago, Breed dreamed that his invention, the airbag, would be installed in every vehicle on the road. He knew that untold thousands of lives would be saved. While most businesses live by the philosophy, "The customer is always right," Breed lived by the opposite. His chief prospective customers – the big three carmakers – refused to have anything to do with this idea. They thought he was full of hot air.

They started rejecting his idea in 1967, despite the public's positive interest. But Breed persisted. He sank everything he had into this invention. Finally, some 17 years later, Congress passed a law that forced automakers to install this lifesaving feature in their vehicles.

Breed, who was named the "1995 Entrepreneur of the Year" by *Inc.* magazine, has now seen thousands survive who would have otherwise died without his invention.

The next time you see the word "airbag" on your steering wheel, remember that great ideas are not always accepted immediately, and overnight success is rarely achieved overnight.

Live and Help Live

An amazing story appeared years ago in a *Guide Post* magazine that affirms a great key to abundant living.

The true story was about a man hiking in the mountains. The man was surprised by a sudden snowstorm and soon lost his way. Since he was not dressed for the frigid temperatures, he knew he had to find shelter quickly or he would freeze to death.

In spite of his efforts, time slipped away and his hands and feet grew numb. He knew his time was short. In his struggle for life, he literally tripped over another man who was almost frozen to death. The hiker had a decision to make: he could either continue on in hopes of saving himself, or he could try to help the stranger in the snow.

He immediately made his decision to help the man. He threw off his wet gloves and knelt beside the man and started massaging his arms and legs. The man soon began to respond and, together, they were able to find help.

Later, he was informed that by helping another he had helped himself! His own numbness disappeared as he massaged the stranger's arms and legs.

Orin Madison summed it up well, "To live and let live is not enough, but to live and help live is not too much."

Self-Government

The doubting citizens of the world at the time looked smugly on – sure that the experiment would fail. The time was the late 1700s. The experiment was self-government, and George Washington was a leader of that experiment. When Washington died in 1799, Congress passed a resolution naming him "first in war, first in peace and first in the hearts of his countrymen."

In his book, *Founding Father*, Richard Brookhiser reflects on how Washington earned such grand tribute.

Washington was a man who believed in character. He served without pay, and led a ragtag army to victory against the mightiest military power of his age.

Washington's life was filled with moral strife. He had a fiery temper, which he restrained with self-discipline. He loved being honored, which he held in check by paying courteous attention to all people.

Washington's primary goal was self-mastery. His guiding philosophies were fortitude, justice, moderation, and the dignity of every person.

We were taught that George Washington was a great leader of an infant nation, but we were not taught that what made Washington great at governing others was how well he governed himself.

Light From Darkness

Little Louis wanted to make saddles just like his dad. He would watch his father's expert work with leather and practice on little scraps given to him.

One day, when his father went across the shop for another tool, little Louis picked up the awl that his father had been using. He jabbed fiercely at the leather trying to make the point go through. As he stabbed the leather, his little fingers lost their grip and the instrument sprang up and struck his left eye.

As a result, he lost the eye and infection soon spread to the other eye. Before long Louis was totally blind.

In those days, blind people were considered less than human and, therefore, were not given any opportunities for learning.

While he was in his teens, Louis heard about a method the military was using to communicate in the dark of night. This technique used a series of dots. Louis set out to refine and enlarge the concept so blind people might learn it as well.

By using a tool very similar to the one that had caused his blindness, Louis punched a series of dots into paper and taught others how to read.

Today, 150 years later, Louis Braille's system is still used to give the light of learning to the blind. He used the very tool that brought him darkness to bring light to millions!

A Life of Risk

Is it possible to live a life without risk? Many people try. Their lives are consumed with hiding from any possibility of failure. But, life is unpredictable in nature; we cannot truly live without taking risks. "To Risk" is a poem that illustrates this theme well:

To laugh is to risk appearing the fool
To weep is to risk appearing sentimental
To reach out for another is to risk involvement
To expose feelings is to risk exposing our true self
To place your ideas, your dreams
before the crowd is to risk loss
To love is to risk not being loved in return
To live is to risk dying
To hope is to risk despair
To try at all is to risk failure
But to risk we must, because the greatest
hazard in life is to risk nothing
The man, the woman, who risk nothing
does nothing
has nothing
is nothing.

– Anonymous

TIME-TESTED VALUES

The Mighty Seed

"Never underestimate the power of a seed!" These words were spoken by H. W. Groves, a British author, who spoke of the magnificent oak castles and cathedrals of England – that still stand strong 500 years after being built.

"How many people could look at a seed and envision these great buildings?" he asked.

America's tallest tree is The Howard Libbey tree in the Redwood Creek Grove. It stands 366 feet high and weighs more than 2,500 tons.

There is a Montezuma Cypress in Oaxaca, Mexico, which has a girth of 113 feet. In 1770, a European Chestnut tree – known as the Chestnut of a Hundred Horses – was recorded to have measured 204 feet in circumference.

Yet the seeds of all these tremendous trees weigh only about 116,000th of an ounce.

Great ideas seem to follow the course of trees and seeds. The idea today that is called great was once regarded as insignificant.

Anyone with eyes can admire the towering tree, but it takes real vision and understanding to stand in awe of a little seed.

Just Lucky

"Some people have all the luck!" How many times have you heard that statement?

After Arnold Palmer once holed out a long shot, somebody remarked how lucky he was.

Palmer responded, "You know, the more I practice, the luckier I get."

While there is no denying the place of odd and fortuitous events in some success stories, luck is a poor foundation for building success – and a poor excuse for not being successful.

I once missed winning a $30,000 car by 1/4 inch in a golf tournament. With a little luck, the ball would have gone in. However, if I had a better swing and game, opportunities like that would be more abundant.

None of us is so foolish to pass up a little good luck when it comes our way; but hopefully, we are not so naive as to sit around and wait for it.

Ralph Waldo Emerson put it aptly, "Shallow men and women believe in luck; wise men and women believe in cause and effect."

If you think you can succeed without causing it, good luck!

Small Beginnings

I remember how awed I was, as a boy, the first time I saw the mighty Mississippi River. The only rivers I had ever seen were maybe 50 -100 yards wide and looked like a neighborhood creek next to the "Mighty Miss."

I wondered where all the water came from. I envisioned some mammoth lake feeding it, but thought, "No, even that would drain out in time." I just could not imagine from where this great water flow originated.

As an adult, I traveled to the little town in Minnesota where the great river starts. What a shock! There was no great lake, no endless reservoir, and no majestic waterfall. Instead, I saw its humble beginning – fed only by dew and small waters. In fact, I am told that there is a point so narrow near its start that you can literally step across the Mississippi.

The lesson of this river is as majestic as the Mississippi itself.

Great things have humble beginnings – they do not become great instantly. It is the daily accumulation of the little things that eventually leads to the great things.

The next time you are overwhelmed at a great challenge, think of that great river. Remember that, at the beginning, it only takes *one step* to get across.

Real Character

John Wooden was, without a doubt, the architect of the greatest college basketball program in history. Coach Wooden led the UCLA Bruins to ten national titles in a 12-year span, including four undefeated seasons.

While many coaches claim that sports is a training ground for character, Wooden disagreed and said, "Sports do not build character, they reveal it."

Wooden is right. Watch people in competitive situations and see their true character surface.

I, for one, thought I had my temper under control until the day I threw my putter in the river!

In his recruiting and coaching, Wooden looked for and focused on character. He said:

"Be more concerned with your character than with your reputation. Your character is what you really are, while your reputation is merely what others think you are!"

Don't Get Even - Get Mad!

Lee Iaccoca is a believer in what a little well-directed anger can accomplish.

In 1979, *The Wall Street Journal* published a scorching editorial criticizing Chrysler's mismanagement and claiming the nearly bankrupt company should be allowed to "die with dignity."

Iaccoca got a ton of mileage out of that quote. It became the cornerstone of his speeches, which aroused the passion needed to save the company. He stated:

"The Wall Street Journal told us to die with dignity. I got mad. Our labor unions, our supplies and our lenders all got mad. We got so mad we banded together, we talked things over, and working together we fixed what was wrong at Chrysler. We doubled our productivity. We rejuvenated our factories. We cut our costs. Wonderful things happen when Americans get mad. I think some well-directed anger can cure most of what's wrong with America today."

Have you been criticized? If so, use criticism as the fuel to drive you. Let it be the impetus to achieve better and greater results.

The Extra Mile at the Last Minute

A friend recently told me about a great experience. He was out of town and needed some articles of clothing, so he went to a mall. He entered a department store almost at closing time – 8:58 p.m. to be exact. He desperately needed some of the items, but he just knew he was going to be turned away.

To his amazement the clerk at this widely known department store said, "Oh, please come in, get whatever you need, and take all the time you need." She then proceeded to start closing the store.

Most people in that situation would have been concerned with only one thing – getting out and getting home. This individual, however, took literally the old adages about "going the extra mile" and "cheerful generosity." And, what an impression she made!

My friend said that whenever he needs anything from a department store, he goes to that store. He is loyal to them because of the way one person treated him.

His observation on the situation was illuminating: "It's hard enough these days to find someone who will go the extra mile," he said. "But to find someone who will go the extra mile at the last minute is rare indeed."

Own Up

A popular concept in the worlds of business and education is the idea of ownership. This idea means that people should have a say in their work, and that they should share in the credit for success and the sharing of the spoils.

Taking ownership is a good concept because it provides incentives for people to get involved in the process and give their best.

There is also a flip side to ownership, however. If we are willing to take control and credit, we must also be willing to take blame for failures.

There is an old saying that fits here: "Success has many fathers, but failure is always an orphan."

People naturally have a hard time owning up to mistakes and admitting culpability. And, even when people admit an error, they have trouble owning up entirely.

Kimberly Johnson wrote, "Never ruin an apology with an excuse."

We can fully understand ownership when we are able to admit and apologize *without* making excuses or sharing blame.

The world has no trouble respecting individuals who are as willing to accept failures as they are successes.

Wanted: Kindness

Chances are you have heard the story of Sylvia Slayton –
better known as the "Meter Maid Granny."
The Cincinnati resident was arrested for the heinous
crime of feeding 15 cents into an expired parking meter –
for someone else's car!
Sylvia said, "Somebody was going to get a ticket and I
was trying to help them avoid that."
The city officials were not pleased. She was arrested
and threatened with four months in jail and $1,000 in fines.

As it turned out, the city of Cincinnati's sting had
uncovered a conspiracy against the municipality of meter
feeders, like Sylvia, who are practicing what they call,
"random acts of kindness;" or, doing unnoticed good
deeds simply to bless others (unnoticed until Sylvia's
arrest, that is).

It seems that an "astute" police officer caught her
violating an obscure 40-year-old law to keep office workers
from hogging storefront spaces.

The "Meter Maid Granny" was trying to save someone
a little grief. It seems that the city had grief to spare.

And, where was Sylvia headed that day when she fed the
meter those fateful 15 cents? On her way to bankruptcy
court! Hmm. Sylvia showed us that we can be broke, but
still have something to give.

Churchill's Battle Plans

In life, we must all fight battles – some bigger than others. Without a proper mental battle plan, many of us are simply unprepared.

Winston Churchill, who is no stranger to victory or defeat, had wise words concerning the proper posture in battle. He said, "In war we must be resolute. In defeat we must be defiant, and, in victory we must be magnanimous."

Churchill later articulated to his nation what it meant to be resolute, "We must never, never, never give up! The will to survive and the will to win cannot be overestimated."

"In defeat we must be defiant." Defeat should not sap our will, but reinforce it. We should embrace an air of defiance when we are defeated, and refuse to believe "that we are not capable of better."

And, what about when we win?

In victory, Churchill said, "magnanimity" is called for. We do not rub it in or revel in our victories. We are far bigger than that. Lincoln's plan was to help restore the South after the Civil War, not punish them. Now, that is magnanimity.

Our daily battles are not quite so severe, but the lessons that guided us so well in the big battles will surely serve us in the little battles.

Remove the Welcome Mat

Why are some people more susceptible to illness than others? Why do some catch every bug that comes around? These were questions that intrigued the great Dr. Albert Schweitzer.

In trying to ascertain answers to these questions, Schweitzer studied not only the habits of the body but of the mind as well. Schweitzer found that many people were susceptible because they extended far too much "hospitality" toward illness. He said, "Disease tends to leave me rather rapidly because it finds so little hospitality in my body."

Schweitzer seems to be saying that people "catch" fewer colds if they stop chasing them.

People spend far too much time talking about illnesses and the latest virus, and imagine themselves being attacked or debilitated. This is why physicians tell us that a high percentage of their patients are called "the walking, worried well."

Schweitzer's advice is pertinent to those who wish to stay well. If you do not desire illness in your house or body, be sure not to leave out the welcome mat!

The Worst Can Bring Out the Best

Gerda Weismann Klein wrote, concerning her Holocaust experience:

> *"Most people think the holocaust camps were like snake pits - that people stepped on each other for survival. It wasn't like that at all. There was kindness, support, understanding.*
>
> *I often talk about a childhood friend of mine, Ilse. She once found a raspberry in the camp and carried it in her pocket all day to present to me that night on a leaf.*
>
> *Imagine a world in which your entire possession is one raspberry and you give it to a friend. Those are the moments I want to remember.*
>
> *People behave nobly under unspeakable circumstances."*

Klein's story is a deeply touching illustration of the profound potential for nobility found in the human soul.

If we choose, we can allow the worst of circumstances to bring out the best in us.

Old Dogs

Back in the winter of 1925, a diphtheria epidemic broke out in Nome, Alaska. The epidemic was adding victims with haste, and the prospects were bleak because of the weather.

Some courageous individuals in Anchorage loaded lifesaving serum on their sleds and headed out with their dogs on the 1,000-mile journey. These human and canine heroes helped to save many lives.

Since 1973, the Iditarod Trail Sled Dog Race has commemorated that historic event. The Iditarod was founded by Joe Redington, Sr., who himself has logged more than 200,000 miles by dog sled, and runs an Iditarod mushing tour business.

Redington ran his first Idtarod at the young age of 56. At 80 years old, he ran – finishing in 36th place – and competitors say he showed no signs of fatigue.

Those same traits of determination and persistence, possessed by the original runners in 1925, have lived on through Redington – a man who never says quit, even to the hands of time.

Redington affirms that it may not be necessary for old dogs to learn new tricks; it is more important that they keep on mushing!

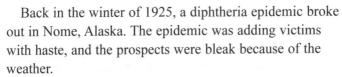

Watching the Polls

Many in our nation believe that we have a leadership crisis. They comment that our so-called leaders do nothing more than watch public opinion polls and then posture themselves toward the popular public opinion. Today's leader, they say, is not a window to the future, but a mirror of whatever people want to see.

Harry Truman eloquently stated:

> *"How far would Moses have gone if he had taken a poll in Egypt? What would Jesus have preached if he had taken a poll in Israel? What would have happened to the Reformation if Martin Luther had taken a poll? It isn't polls or public opinion of the moment that counts. It is right and wrong and leadership."*

Truman put the focus back where it belongs in leadership. Listening to the mob is dangerous because mob opinions shift quickly and radically.

Each of us must determine what is right, just, and good. We must not lead by the polls; but, instead, be tethered to the poles of wisdom and truth.

Leadership is not about following opinion – it is leading toward truth.

Good Reminders

All of us, occasionally, need a few good reminders of the things we believe in. William Kirkpatrick wrote:

> "*Martin Luther King, Jr. was able to overcome the entrenched culture of Jim Crow in the South not because he had invented a new set of principles, but because he appealed to a tradition that both preceded and transcended Jim Crow.*
>
> *When he attended Cozer Theological Seminary, he immersed himself in the writings of Plato, Aristotle, Mill and Locke.*
>
> *In his speeches he referred to Lincoln, to the Declaration of Independence, to Negro-spirituals, to Moses and the Promised Land."*

King, in short, was the bearer of a tradition. He was able to mobilize white as well as black Americans because he reminded them of what they already believed about justice and human decency. His demand was not that America creates a new morality, but that it lives up to its best traditions and beliefs.

Kirkpatrick's words remind us that today's world problems do not require brand-new codes and values, but a return look at some ancient and time-tested truths.

"Sweet 16"

Larry was excited about his daughter's 16th birthday party coming up on Friday. A very special "sweet 16" celebration was planned with relatives coming from many miles away.

Then, Larry's boss called: "Larry, we need you to be in Boston for a meeting on Friday."

"But," Larry hesitated, "it is my daughter's 16th birthday. We have a big party planned. I've got to keep my priorities straight."

"That's right," his boss responded, "you need to keep your priorities straight. Without this job, how will you feed your family? Be in Boston, or else!"

Larry had risen to the level of vice-president for this large corporation. He was making great money, but he recognized that this was the beginning of the end.

His boss' threat displayed how his corporation had counterfeited meaningful values. So, Larry found another position for a smaller company at half the pay, but he felt better about what he was doing.

Larry missed that bitter "sweet 16" birthday party, but he rearranged his life so that he would never miss another.

A test of our values – although never easy – is what ultimately defines us as people.

100 and Counting

Scientists are taking a real interest in the number 100; or, rather, those people who live to that number.

Today, there are more than 50,000 Americans over the age of 100, which is triple the number back in 1980.

Many of these centenarians still live on their own and continue to be active in their communities. Very few waste their time wishing they had lived their lives differently.

Haya El Nassar writes about the incredible story of 104-year-old Angeline Strandal of Quincy, Illinois. Each morning, after rising at 8:45 a.m., she makes her bed, cooks breakfast, washes dishes, bathes, and then takes a walk.

She has voted in every presidential election since women won the right to vote in 1920. She is an avid baseball fan who remembers the last time the Red Sox won the World Series with a pitcher named Babe Ruth in 1918.

She has outlived her husband by 66 years so far. "I don't feel old," she said, "but I'll soon be 105. I guess I am getting old." But, she quickly adds, "I keep busy. I don't sit there and say I can't get up."

She shares a simple key to her longevity: "I just ask God for another day and He gives it to me."

Door Openers

Two customers – a perfect contrast of one another – arrived at a business counter at the same time.

The first was a man finely dressed, bespectacled, and possessed an air of self-importance. The second was a lady, somewhat plain, but neat in appearance, and possessed an air of humility.

The clerk addressed her first, "May I help you?"

Before she could respond, the woman was promptly cut off by the man. "Excuse me," he informed the clerk with perfect enunciation, "I believe I was here first and I'm in quite a hurry."

The woman said, "That's fine," and politely stepped back.

Irritated, the clerk said to the woman, "That's OK, I'm sure I can help you in short order."

The clerk then turned to the man and crisply stated, "I'll be right with you."

The story reminds me of an observation made by Justice Clarence Thomas, "Good manners will open doors that the best education cannot."

Those who have gathered knowledge and credentials to the degree that they now believe they are above the laws of common courtesy, have fallen prey to extreme stupidity.

People are more impressed with kindness than with knowledge. Doors open quickly – not to those impressed with themselves, but to those impressed with the importance of others.

Fix It As Soon As You See It

Al and his partner made a serious mistake in preparing the foundation for a construction project. The footings were not on solid enough ground – they needed to dig deeper.

Because they were facing the pressure of several other jobs and deadlines, they decided to go ahead and build the addition anyway – and hope for the best.

Eventually, the inevitable happened. The foundation settled and shifted, which caused the walls and ceilings to crack and separate. Not surprisingly, the customers were irate and called their lawyer.

Al and his partner were wrong and they paid for it. Not only did they lose the lawsuit, their insurance rates skyrocketed and their reputation suffered irreparable damage. They eventually were forced out of business.

The time to fix mistakes is as soon as we see them. Mistakes only get the best of those who refuse to confront them. While it may seem like a lot of work at the time to undo and redo, it is nowhere near the trouble that mistakes bring when left to themselves.

Everyone makes mistakes; however, people of integrity are not afraid to confront them – immediately!

What Lies Within You

Oliver Wendell Holmes wrote: "What lies before us and what lies behind us are tiny matters compared to what lies within us."

We spend so much time worrying about our future. "Do we have what it takes?" or "What will happen?" or "Can we make it?"

Some spend even more time looking in the rear-view mirror. "Why did I do that?" or "Why didn't that work out?" or "What is wrong with me?"

The most beneficial focus, according to Holmes, is neither ahead nor behind – but *within.*

Within us we have the resources to process and parlay our past into a school of discovery and improvement. Our past cannot change, but it can help change us.

Within us we have the power to change our attitudes, behavior, and outlook in a way that will positively change our future course.

What has happened, and what will happen, are tiny matters when compared with what we can make happen!

Win by Losing

In his book, *The Secret Power Within*, martial arts expert and actor Chuck Norris writes about how he handled a potentially violent confrontation.

Norris was in a small Texas bar having a beer in the corner booth. A large man walked up and told Norris that he was sitting in his booth.

Norris didn't like his tone or his implicit threat, but he said nothing and moved to another booth.

The big fellow started coming toward him again. "Here it comes," Norris thought, "a local tough guy out to make a name for himself by taking on Chuck Norris."

When the man arrived at the new booth, he said, "You're Chuck Norris."

Norris nodded and said, "Yes."

"You could have whipped me back there," the man said slowly. "Why didn't you?"

"What would it have proved?" Norris asked.

The man thought it over for a moment and then offered his hand. "No hard feelings?" he asked.

"None," Norris replied, and then shook his hand.

Norris writes, "Not only did I avoid a confrontation, I made a friend. I won by losing!"

Too often we think we must conquer to win. But sometimes – like Norris – we can win by losing.

Get Your Hands Dirty

What do dirty hands have to do with happy hearts?
Writer Jim Sollisch has some interesting insight on that
question. He writes:

*"Most of the really happy people I know get their
hands dirty all the time. They garden or cook or
refinish furniture. They touch basic materials that are
closer to life than objects pre-fabbed, preprogrammed,
preprocessed and predisposed to minimize tactile
stimulation."*

Sollisch goes on to tell about the joy he and his father
experienced when they built their own canoe – instead
of plunking down a few hundred dollars to buy one.

Some people long to have enough money to have
everything done for them. But, as many have discovered,
they are missing the point. It is the creator, the doer, the
fixer, and the builder who possesses the greater joy. For
they have put their hands to the task and helped change
objects from a nonexistent or broken state to one of
usefulness and beauty.

That which we nurture with our hands will bring
happiness to the heart. A key to life enjoyment, then,
is a willingness to get our hands dirty.

Passing the Test

Cabby David Hacker had just finished his ten-hour shift in Las Vegas, when he spotted a bulging wallet on the back seat of his cab.

The wallet held $25,000, which is what David Hacker makes in a year of ten-hour shifts, six days a week.

"This is it," Hacker thought. "This is a test from above."

You see, awhile back, Hacker had some serious health problems and he told God if He would help him through this time of trouble, he would do his best to return the favor.

He decided that this was his chance. So, he looked in the wallet and found some credit cards that identified the wallet's owner as "Mr. Lance Dykes." Hacker thought that the man might be a passenger he had picked up at Bally's. Sure enough, he found Mr. Dykes at a roulette wheel in that casino.

Almost speechless, Dykes told Hacker that he figured the wallet was long gone – especially given that he had lost it in Las Vegas. He thanked Hacker over and over and handed him a $5,000 cash reward, food, clothes, and a whole week of living the high life.

Hacker met his test and passed it with flying colors. He lives by a bigger and better rule than "finder's keepers - loser's weepers."

Good Values Linger

Ashton Kutcher is amazed at how ungrateful some people can be when success comes their way. Kutcher, one of the young stars of the TV sitcom, *That 70's Show,* is grateful for everything that has come his way. He thinks that his Midwestern roots have something to do with that attitude.

Kutcher grew up in Amana, Iowa, and vividly recalls the many jobs he worked as a youth: sweeping up dust at a General Mills plant, washing dishes at various restaurants, and skinning deer in a butcher shop.

He thinks his Iowa background may have contributed to his intolerance of people who have grown up in Hollywood's showy lifestyle. Kutcher states:

> *"They're making umpteen thousand dollars a week and they're not happy with it. I'm like, 'How can you not be happy?' I was never able to buy a new car. I washed dishes. You can't believe how ungrateful people can be."*

Kutcher's comments strike a troubling attitudinal vein in our society: The more people have, the more they want – and the less happy they are with what they have. The result is that gratitude is in short supply.

It is refreshing to hear a young actor and role model to youth who demonstrates such gratitude.

Kutcher is proof that good values do linger.

Hang Onto Seeds

Each day we get a chance to collect some very important philosophical seeds – little thoughts, ideas, phrases, quotes, or proverbs. These seeds we hear and read can become quite instrumental to our mental health, sense of purpose, and ability to deal with stress.

Start looking for little phrases that click with you. Put those words in places where you can rediscover them once in awhile. I try to surround myself with wise words because it seems I can never learn enough soon enough.

Certain sayings can act as billboards in our brains and help us to focus on a direction and fortitude. One of my favorites is by George Eliot, "It's never too late to be what you always could have been" (a reminder to use your abilities and pursue your dreams).

These seeds, or billboards of the brain, do grow as we ponder them. They can direct us down rewarding paths and are useful in chasing off thoughts of foolishness and anxiety.

Make sure you plant philosophical seeds. Water them now and then – and watch yourself grow.

TIME-TESTED VALUES

The Power of Humility

Businesses and organizations that possess a positive environment can usually trace their culture of good feeling to a basic value. Whether this value is humility, decisiveness, or open communication, it must be stressed often by the company's leaders.

Geophysicist Conrad Schlumberger built his company on one simple virtue: humility. Not only was humility central to the growth of his company, but accelerated his growth as a scientist.

Schlumberger believes that learning and growth can be achieved only through humility. He states, "If you think you know the answers, where is the motivation to learn?" His presumption was that you need humility to listen to your customers, employees, and associates.

In his book, *The Art of Corporate Success*, Ken Auletta writes:

> *"Schlumberger listened every chance he got and viewed feedback from others as a key step in research. Learning gave him a sense of optimism that never failed him. He inbred others with that optimism."*

Schlumberger's story reveals a rarely acknowledged link in the chain of success – the link between humility and optimism. When we are willing to learn and willing to listen, there is always the hope of finding an answer, of forging alliances, and of discovering the keys that will unlock opportunities.

The Greatest Generation

According to anchorman Tom Brokaw, it is time to get your children to sit down and listen to the stories that their grandparents have to tell about their struggles and accomplishments in America.

In his book, *The Greatest Generation,* Brokaw makes a compelling argument that our parents and grandparents, who survived the Great Depression and held off Nazi and Japanese aggression in WWII, are the greatest generation of Americans to ever live.

Their feats, Brokaw contends, eclipse even those of our founding fathers and Abraham Lincoln's generation.

Most of these people were in their teens and early 20's, but gave selflessly to our society. When they came home from the war effort, they settled down to build our great highway system, go nose to nose with communism, send men to the moon, and defeat polio.

Brokaw states, "Through modesty and pain, most chose not to talk about the struggles of their youth" and are now dying at a rate of 100 a day. He believes that, if we are to understand America, we must hear from them.

He writes, "These people stepped up and saved the world. Younger people will be astonished. They'll look at their grandparents in a different way."

Brokaw's message is similar to Steven Spielberg's message in *Saving Private Ryan.* We all owe so much to this great generation.

From the Heart

In a time when so many acts of good will are done for the cameras, and when wealthy celebrities' acts of charity are a mere pittance of what they are truly able to give, it is quite refreshing to hear about a man like Charles Feeney.

I hesitate to write about Mr. Feeney's benevolent heart because he has spent his entire life shunning such publicity.

You see, it was revealed that Mr. Feeney has given away most of his $4 billion fortune to hospitals, schools, and other groups – and he did it all anonymously.

The recent sale of his businesses required that he reveal where this vast sum of money went (again, that figure was $4 billion!). And yet, Mr. Feeney does not own a home or a car, always flies economy, and wears a $15 watch.

Mr. Feeney's comment: "I simply decided I had enough money. It doesn't drive my life. I'm a what-you-see-is-what-you-get kind of guy."

Mr. Charles Feeney, we like what we see.

To quote an old verse, "Those who give for all to see already have their reward, but those who give in secret shall be rewarded openly."

Mr. Feeney's charity is an encouragement to all of us to give from the heart!

New Priorities

After losing his mother to cancer, Fred Silverman decided to use his talents to help encourage those diagnosed with cancer. The result was a PBS documentary entitled *Living with Cancer*, which Silverman co-wrote, directed, and produced.

Silverman's documentary notes the dramatic change in attitude that cancer brings to many. "Many of them have such a zest for life," he says. "They realize how sacred life really is, and they value it far more than others who have never faced a life-threatening situation."

One cancer survivor put it this way, "For the first time, my nose was up against the glass of mortality. And you're scared right down to the bottom of your toes."

Another cancer survivor noted that a diagnosis of cancer usually results in a change in priorities. She said, "If there is a gift to cancer, it is in making you aware how precious each day is and in raising your consciousness to the point where you live life better. It's too bad that sometimes it takes a kind of jolt to bring us that awareness."

For many, it takes a real threat to focus on what really matters. But, those new priorities are available to us anytime we choose.

"Awesome, Baby!"

Dick Vitale of the *ESPN* television network is "Awesome, baby!" – and that is Awesome with a capital "A!"

In a world filled with duplicitous public figures and personalities, Vitale's "what-you-see-is-what-you-get" persona is refreshing.

When Vitale comes to town, he does not hide in the penthouse suite on the top floor of luxury hotels. He is seen walking down Main Street, shaking hands, signing autographs, and conversing with anyone who wants to talk to him. Those who have met "Dicky V." agree – this guy is for real.

Vitale says, "When I was young my parents explained to me that if you are good to people and you're enthusiastic in life, good things will happen for you. I've always lived by that."

Enthusiasm. Exuberance. Expression. Excitement. Vitale has it – and he spreads it around like wildfire. Some people are annoyed by his excitability on television, but I believe true passion is in short enough supply in this world, so let's not extinguish those who have it.

Vitale is simply in love with Life – and, that is Life with a capital "L," baby!

Pictures for Daddy

One of the truly satisfying pleasures in my life is the collection of pictures that my daughter, Sophia, has drawn for me. These masterpieces – marked indelibly in my mind – adorn my car, bedroom, and office.

Whenever I am away on a trip and I talk to her on the phone, she tells me, "I miss you, Daddy, and I'm drawing you a picture."

I have learned a great deal from her pictures. There are cats and dogs, trees and lakes, the sun, moon, and stars, and lots of people. And there is one thing I always notice: everyone and everything is smiling – and in a big way!

Come to think of it, about every picture I have ever seen by a child has people smiling. Did you know that children laugh 30 times more than adults do? And, we call this growing up!

The lesson I learn from this is that happiness is our natural state, and unhappiness is learned behavior.

Sophia's pictures have taught me that there is beauty in everything if we look for it. Her drawings remind me that we live in a big, wonderful world, and that Daddy can smile and be very happy – if Daddy wants to.

Exercise of Prayer

Science, it seems, is starting to catch up with Religion. For centuries, the two disciplines have been at odds in their views of the world and the universe. In recent years, however, Science has begun to study the phenomena of Religion and spiritual disciplines.

Recent studies indicate that attending religious services may actually improve our physical health and psychological well-being.

The Journal of Gerontology reported on a 12-year study of 2,812 individuals, aged 65 and older, from Protestant, Catholic, Jewish, and other religious backgrounds. Among other things, the study noted that religious involvement could influence positive changes in physical health.

Dr. Herbert Benson, of Harvard Medical School, was one of the first researchers to study the health benefits of prayer. In his study, Benson found that prayer was effective in stimulating healthful, physiological changes in the body - what he called the "relaxation response."

Benson also discovered that when subjects combined exercise and prayer, their bodies became more efficient.

Science now teaches what Religion has always taught: Prayer is not only healthy, it also is good exercise.

Einsteinium Success

Albert Einstein's phenomenal achievements as a scientist overshadowed his tremendous erudition and skill as a philosopher.

He was troubled about the way young people in his day were – specifically in the manner success was defined. Einstein wrote:

"We should guard against teaching a young man or woman with the idea that success is the aim of life, for a successful person normally receives from his peers an incomparably greater portion than the services he has been able to render them deserved. The value of a person resides in what he gives and not in what he is capable of receiving.

The most important motive for study at school, at the university, and in life is the pleasure of working and thereby obtaining results that will serve the community. The most important task for an educator (or parent) is to waken and encourage these psychological forces in a young man or woman. Such a basis alone can lead to the joy of possessing one of the most precious assets in the world - knowledge or artistic skill."

Einstein hit the nail on the head of where our society errs, "Success is best measured by our ability to give, not our ability to receive."

Your Second Job

Albert Schweitzer was truly one of the remarkable figures of the 20th century. By the age of 30, he had already become Europe's premier organist, an acclaimed biographer, and a first-rate theologian. He then decided to study medicine in order to devote his life to helping people in Africa. He knew some things about making each life count. Schweitzer wrote:

> *"People often say, 'I would like to do some good in the world, but with my responsibilities at home and in business, my nose is always to the grindstone. I am sunk in my own petty affairs and there is no chance for my life to mean anything.'"*

Schweitzer advocated getting a second job – but probably not the kind you think. He called the second job a career for the spirit. By finding a way to help others, people actually help themselves.

Schweitzer said that what our modern world lacks most is "people who occupy themselves with the needs of other people."

Volunteering with a league or the local charity, church, or service organization "is a way," Schweitzer said, "to put our reserve energies to work."

If you are looking for meaning, you may find it in your second job – and "the pay you get," Schweitzer said, "is the privilege of getting to do it!"

That's the Truth, Teacher!

Four teenagers decided to go to school a little late and avoid a first hour test. They met together for breakfast and moseyed into the school.

The teacher, whose test they missed, caught them in the hall and pulled them into his room.

"Where have you been?" the teacher demanded.

"We're sorry, " their brave leader explained, "but we ride together to school every day, and it was my turn to drive and I got a flat tire on the way to school. I made these guys late."

"Is that right?" the teacher asked the others.

"Sure is," they all agreed.

"Since you missed the test first period," he told them, "I'll have to give you a shortened version. Each of you take out a pencil and paper, sit in the four corners of this room, and answer just one question, 'Which tire went flat?'"

This story reminds me of the quote by George Plunkett, "Never tell a lie unless lying is one of your strong points."

Money Talks

Sure, money talks, but what exactly is it saying? Bob Dylan once said, "Money doesn't talk – it swears."

How much money would it take to get you to compromise your values or principles? This is the very question researchers Patterson & Kim asked in their landmark book, *The Day America Told the Truth*.

They set the price at $10 million, and then set out to see what people would be willing to do to get it. Here are their results:

- Twenty-five percent of respondents said they would abandon their entire family, become a prostitute for a week, or abandon their religion.
- Seven percent said they would kill a stranger.

Next, Patterson & Kim decided to lower the price. What they found was that the respondents said they would do the same things for $5 million, then $4 million, and $3 million. It was at $2 million that they began to have a change of heart!

Patterson & Kim concluded that the "going rate" for the American conscience is at about $2 million.

Their findings should give us all enough cause to question our own values and look deep down inside to see how easily we could rationalize our way out of them.

A simple formula for measuring the strength of our values is to determine the price someone would have to pay to get us to change those values.

Detecting Counterfeits

How do you detect a counterfeit? I am not referring to counterfeit currency, but to counterfeit ideas and opportunities.

A bank teller once explained to me the training she received to detect counterfeit money. Surprisingly, she was not trained to recognize forgeries. Instead, she was given volumes of the "real article" so that she would learn the feel so well that she would automatically stop when she detected a bill that did not "feel" quite right. The bill in question would then go through visual scrutiny to determine its legitimacy.

People are often approached with opportunities and ideas that look and sound like good deals; but, like the forged money, do not "feel" quite right. Chances are good that:

1. If something doesn't feel quite right, it isn't.
2. If it sounds too good to be true, it is.
3. If the other person has nothing to lose, then the risk is all yours.

We are more prone to be fooled by our eyes and ears than we are by our inner sense of feel.

And, remember, the best defense for error is to be well acquainted with the truth.

In Stitches

Dr. Stubbs is not your average doctor and he certainly does not look like your average doctor: He has a big, red nose, a painted face, and size 18EEE shoes. He looks more like a clown than a doctor; in fact, he is a clown and he heads up the Clown Care Unit in New York City.

Dr. Stubbs' real name is Michael Christensen and he has seen enough to convince him that humor is a healer. Now, scientists are going to study this phenomenon.

Christensen, who lost a brother to pancreatic cancer, set out on a yearlong investigation of clowns visiting children in hospitals to find out if laughter truly is the best medicine. He is a firm believer that it is.

Christensen has seen firsthand how powerful a treatment a "red-nose transplant" or a "chocolate-milk transfusion" can be.

So far, there is little medical explanation for why a kid gets better after watching Dr. Stubbs sit on a whoopee cushion, but he has seen it happen.

Christensen – or Dr. Stubbs – has discovered that, no matter how sick patients are, it is important to keep them "in stitches."

The Richest Legacy

Each year, the Heisman trophy is given to America's premier collegiate football player. In 1939, the winner of that coveted prize was the legendary runningback from the University of Iowa, Niles Kinnick.

Kinnick's legend extended far beyond his exploits on the field. He gave his life in WWII and was posthumously decorated. Iowa's football stadium today bears his namesake.

Greater than all of his accomplishments, however, was this man's honor.

On the last day of his award-winning season, the Hawkeyes were playing for the Big-Ten Championship. With just seconds to go in the game, the Hawkeyes were down and driving to their opponent's goal line.

Kinnick took the hand-off and headed to the end zone for what would be the winning score. Just as he hit the goal line, he fumbled. The officials could not decide if he had crossed the goal before the fumble – and everyone knew that the championship was on the line.

The officials then did something unheard of: Knowing Niles Kinnick to be a man above reproach, they asked him if he had crossed the goal. Kinnick replied that he was 99 percent sure that he had *not* crossed the goal line.

Iowa lost the championship.

Why is Kinnick's legacy so great? In the words of William Shakespeare, "No legacy is so rich as honesty."

TIME-TESTED VALUES

Speed: The Enemy of Progress?

They keep putting faster processors in our computers. They build faster planes and quicker systems for getting everything done. Yet, the lives of most people continue to move at a frantic pace as they try to keep up with the latest speed standard.

I believe that speed is overrated. Quicker is not always better. Because we place so much emphasis on "faster," we pay less attention to "better," and quality gets lost in the race to a blurred finish line.

Many folks have high blood pressure because their blood is simply trying to keep up with their feet.

Today, more than ever, we need to heed the words of the ageless poem, "Persevere:"

> *The fisher who draws in his net*
> *   too soon won't have any fish to sell.*
> *The child who shuts up his book too soon*
> *   won't learn any lessons well.*
> *If you would have your learning stay,*
> *   be patient – don't learn too fast.*
> *The man who travels a mile each day*
> *   may get around the world at last.*

Speed is the blinding culprit that keeps us from enjoying the journey.

EQ

According to Daniel Golemn, author of *Emotional Intelligence*, it is great to possess intelligence (IQ); however, it is even greater to possess emotional intelligence (EQ).

Goleman believes that many people who have a great deal of ability continue to sabotage their own success because of a lack of emotional intelligence. They have not learned the proper responses to people and adverse situations.

One of the emotional keys Goleman writes about is "the ability to empathize." Here are two examples:

- *Scenario #1*: You and your wife are having a disagreement. You listen to her concerns with empathy, and you strike a compromise, which results in a reduction of stress in your home.
- *Scenario #2*: You go into a negotiation. You have already looked at the issues from the other party's point of view. You bring reasonable and fair requests to the meeting.

The ability to empathize simply means we look at matters from the other person's point of view. We have to give up the idea that our view is always right. This is called, "emotional intelligence."

If you ask executives or managers why they have had to fire employees, they will most likely give you the following reasons: they didn't listen; they wouldn't change; they were hostile; and they just didn't empathize with those around them.

Your IQ is a matter of record, but your EQ is in constant recording. Direct your destiny by directing your emotions!

Anonymous Angel

When the ravaging floods hit North Dakota and Minnesota, residents were blessed and encouraged by the generosity of an "Anonymous Angel" who gave $15 million to help.

The anonymity of this angel did not last long, however, as the media sought to uncover her identity. They discovered that the angel was Joan Kroc, heiress to the McDonald's fortune and one of the 400 wealthiest individuals in America. Kroc carries with her what one writer describes as, "The strange yoke of both privileges and responsibility borne by the enormously wealthy."

Kroc's goal was not to be acknowledged, but to help people as fast as possible. She told government officials she wanted to cut through all the red tape that often bogs down the government.

Her generous gift inspired others to give as well. Although some people who gave $100 may have sacrificed more on a relative basis, it was her example that started a huge flow of relief. Soon, another "angel" gave $5 million.

Joan Kroc's example should be noted and praised. She simply saw a need and wanted to meet it – no strings attached.

Heroes

I have heard some folks say that a big problem for kids today is that they do not have enough real heroes. They are growing up in an age where famous athletes are saying, "I'm not a role model" or "I don't want to be your role model."

Some are asserting that this dearth of direction is about to take an entire generation astray.

I recently asked the question, "Who is your role model, and why?" to a group of high school students. An onlooker would have been amazed. One by one they stood up and told about great and extraordinary people they admired and whose examples they followed.

They spoke of the powerful lessons they had learned and of values such as respect, hard work, persistence, creativity, generosity, tolerance, and responsibility.

Any skeptic hearing this would have been encouraged about our world's future – if these young people were to have anything to do with it.

And who were their heroes that taught them these great lessons? You may have heard of them – they were their moms, dads, grandpas and grandmas, aunts and uncles.

These heroes were people they watch in action *every day.*

Work Worth Doing

Sometimes when I need a good laugh, I pick up the newspaper, and instead of reading the comics, I read the business opportunity ads. Some of them never fail to amuse me.

Their bait includes such tempting promises as, "Do nothing and get rich!" or "Sit and collect checks!" or "Let others work for you!" These alluring advertisements are usually followed by an 800 number, or in some cases, a 900 number.

What great fiction – promises of wealth and contentment without hard work! M. M. Cowan said, "Work is man's greatest function. He is nothing, he can do nothing, achieve nothing, fulfill nothing without working."

I am reminded of the irony I saw in a television interview with a welfare recipient who was bemoaning his loss of benefits: "Listen," he protested, "I worked hard to collect that check!"

Indeed. Nothing satisfies quite like hard work. The wise individual knows that promises of profit without hard work are empty and futile.

Good Judgment

The year was 1787. The event was the convening of the First Continental Congress. Their job was to establish a rock-solid constitution for the new Republic.

For weeks, they debated and negotiated over the document that would set the compass for the future of the new nation. They debated heatedly over whether the Houses of Congress should be represented equally, or be based on population. At this point, they hit a virtual stalemate – everyone was ready to go back home without a constitution.

Franklin stepped in to work out a compromise and gave this speech to his fellow founding fathers:

"The older I get, the more inclined I am to doubt my own judgment. I am inclined at times to believe, like all men, that my view, based on evidence I have seen must be right. But, I have too many times, received enlightenment or information after such a judgment sufficient enough to change my view."

Franklin admitted that he, too, doubted the wisdom of some of the points in the constitution; but at the same time, he doubted the infallibility of his judgment.

A compromise was met, and the greatest governmental constitution in history was enacted.

Sometimes it is good judgment to doubt your own judgment.

Longevity

Modern geneticists are looking fervently through their microscopes for the keys to longevity.

They are probably looking in the wrong place and through the wrong glass.

They ought to be looking through a telescope at the remote Abcasian culture in the mountains of Southern Russia.

The Abcasians boast five times more centenarians than any culture on earth. They may be the only culture on our planet to have a word for "great-great-great-grandparent" and no common word for "old."

They are simple farming people who tend tea fields and they subsist on 1,500-calorie diets of vegetables, nuts, fruits, and a little meat.

The Abcasians do not practice mandatory retirement. Certificates are regularly awarded to people who are working in the fields at 100-years-old. One lady, at 109, logged in 49 full working days during a recent summer.

The Abcasian culture values longevity above material gain. They practice a healthy lifestyle instead of a greedy one. The older people become, the more important they become.

Americans are obsessed with longevity and seem to overlook one key: cultures who live the longest are those who pay greater respect to the elderly, not less.

"What's He Worth?"

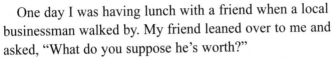

One day I was having lunch with a friend when a local businessman walked by. My friend leaned over to me and asked, "What do you suppose he's worth?"

The question caught me off-guard. First of all, it was none of my business. Second of all, my idea of a person's worth was certainly different than his.

"It depends how you measure it," I answered.

I had spent a number of years answering calls on a crisis line. I remember talking to people, who despite their wealth, felt their lives were worthless. I had come to the conclusion that a checkbook was a poor barometer of a person's value in this world. If this isn't the case, you'd have to say that Mother Teresa is worthless.

Magazines publish lists of the world's ten richest, but never the world's ten most generous (which is probably a good thing because truly giving people do not crave attention for their good deeds).

Your net worth can be immediately increased – not by what you take out of this world, but by what you put back in.

TIME-TESTED VALUES

Other books by Mitch Anthony

General Audiences:
The New Retirementality
Seven Reasons to Keep On Living
Suicide: Knowing When Your Teen Is At Risk

Professional Books:
StorySelling for Financial Advisors
Making Client Connections
Your Clients for Life
Selling with Emotional Intelligence

Mitch Anthony's books are available at special quantity discounts to use as premiums and sales promotions, or for use in corporate training programs.

For more information, visit our website at:
www.mitchanthony.com

Or, call Advisor Insights Inc. at (507) 282-2723.